IT'S OUR WORLD—CHANGE IT!

A LEADERSHIP JOURNEY

aMAZE!

THE TWISTS AND TURNS OF GETTING ALONG

START

GIRL SCOUTS OF THE USA

girl scouts

SENIOR DIRECTOR, PROGRAM RESOURCES: Suzanne Harper
ART DIRECTOR: Douglas Bantz
WRITERS: Monica Shah, Mariam MacGregor, Alison Hill
CONTRIBUTORS: Laura Birnbaum, Kelli Martin, Jessica Slote
ILLUSTRATOR: Jennifer Kalis
DESIGNER: Parham Santana

MIX
Paper from responsible sources
FSC® C011825

contents

LIFE IS FULL OF AMAZING EQUATIONS:

Me=limitless possibilities

You=limitless possibilities + another viewpoint

Me + You = interactions of boundless possibilities^2

Me + You x Both Our Networks = Diplomats^{10}

Diplomats^{10} x Millions More Around the World = peace on the planet, or at least a far better world

LIFE IS ALSO FULL OF MAZES

Twists and turns, dead-ends and U-turns.
Every day is a maze of possibilities.
In the maze of life, you encounter everything
that's fun and confusing and funny and difficult
about finding your way.

A maze can represent all of life—
or just one important experience.
Once you maneuver through one maze,
there's usually another waiting for you
right behind it.

Mazes mean possibilities.
So go ahead, choose a path. Get in the game!

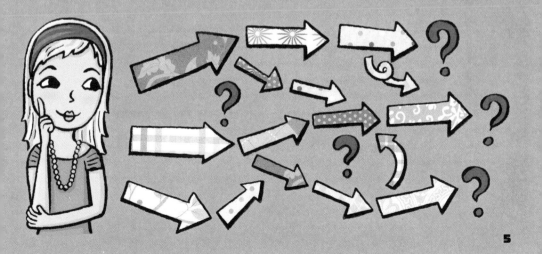

THE TWISTS AND TURNS IN YOUR

EVERYDAY MAZES

Belonging

GIGGLE FITS

Frenemies

School

BFFs

Gossip

JEALOUSY

Embarrassing moments

Clubs

Cliques

REJECTION

Fitting in

Speaking up

So you guessed it:

aMAZE is a journey about relationships—yours and the rest of the world's, or at least some of those right around you.

Relationships don't stand still. They shift and slide and sputter—a little like the way the parts of a virtual game move around each time you play. Just as you figure out, say, one really good friendship, another one changes right before your eyes.

aMAZE is your chance to sort out everything you already know about managing the twists and turns of friendships. It's also your opportunity to gather new tips and strategies for interacting with all the people in your life—and those beyond it. By the time you wind your way through this amazing journey called aMAZE, you may be quite the diplomat! And world peace? Well, just take it one relationship at a time!

A Maze of Your Own

Your life is your own! Show all its twists and turns below—regular everyday ones and special ones.

Maybe you can think of times when you tried really hard to work something out with others—resolved a conflict with a sibling, said "sorry" to a friend, reached out to someone beyond your usual circle. How does it feel to interact at your very best?

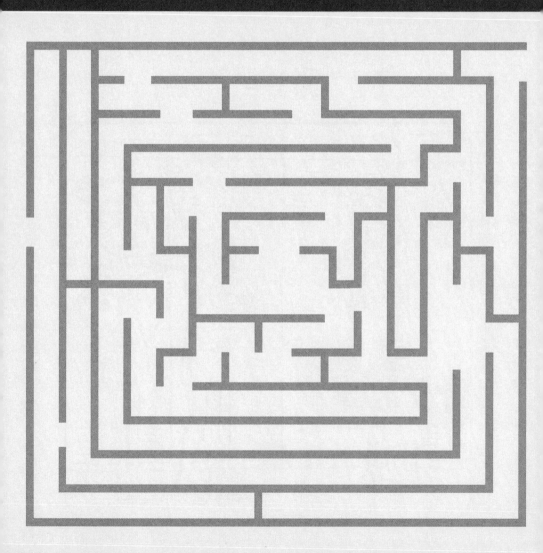

Rewards and Awards

The best rewards in life often come from within. As you work your way through aMAZE, amazing the world with your relationship savvy, you can earn some official Girl Scout awards, too. Go after one, two, or all three—the choice is yours. Here are the awards and how to earn them:

Interact Award: Reach Out a Little

(You + Who? = Improving the World, One Relationship at a Time)

Interact Challenges are small actions you can do in your daily life to improve relationships—yours and those around you. This journey offers nine challenges to "interact." Do three of them to earn the Interact Award. Check out the full list of Interact Challenges on page 12 and chart your progress as you go.

Diplomat Award: Use Your Relationship Savvy to Improve Your World

(You + Who + Who + Who Else = Improving the World Many Relationships at a Time)

To earn the Diplomat Award, create and do a Take Action Project aimed at building more positive and peaceful relationships in the world around you. Maybe your project can have some lasting power in your community—or get passed forward by others. All the tips and tools you'll need start on page 112.

Peacemaker Award: Commit to Keep It Going

(You + How Many Others = World Peace?)

As you travel through aMAZE, you'll gain valuable relationship skills and strategies. Choose those most important to you for your Peacemaker Kit. You'll find "Peacemaker Kit" sections throughout this book. Fill them in. Earn the Peacemaker Award by committing to use these skills to create peace in the world around you— even if just in your school hallways. Go ahead, let peace begin with you!

LEAD ON!

The twists, turns, and awards of aMAZE follow the Girl Scout philosophy of leadership. That means you will:

DISCOVER what's important to you,
CONNECT with your Girl Scout crew and others in the larger community, and
TAKE ACTION to make the world a better place.

Your Trusted Adult

Most trips you take involve trusted adults. This one is no different. After all, thinking about, talking about, and building relationships can be tough stuff. So, what adult in your life can be there for you—a parent, an aunt, older cousin, sibling? Let someone know you're on a journey all about relationships and may need some time to talk. It's a mark of intelligence to reach out. Plus, you'll probably find that people love to share insights they've gained from their own relationships.

> *Just as treasures are uncovered from the earth,*
> *so virtue appears from good deeds,*
> *and wisdom appears from a pure and peaceful mind.*
> *To walk safely through the maze of human life,*
> *one needs the light of wisdom and the guidance of virtue.*
>
> —*Buddha*

YOU and YOUR aMAZE MaTeS

No road is long with good company.
—*Turkish proverb*

Venture through this book any time you want. Test your smarts on the quizzes and questions. Try some of the tips in your own relationships. You'll gain more—and have more fun—if you involve your friends or team up with a Girl Scout group and travel through aMAZE together. Just remember:

- ***Learning is good.*** So share your discoveries: Role-model, lead, and support other girls around you.

- ***Honesty is best.*** Show your feelings and trust your gut. That's the only way to strengthen relationships.

- ***Connect with your team.*** Making it through a maze isn't always smooth, but it's a good way to build unity. Challenge each other— with encouragement.

- ***Have fun!*** Relationships, and leadership, thrive on laughter and creativity.

GOT MAZE MANIA?

Journey through a life-size maze with friends. They're all around the country—corn mazes in autumn, permanent hedge mazes, and stone and dirt labyrinths.

No life-size mazes near you? Visit a miniature golf course and try getting your ball through the zigzag paths while avoiding the pitfalls and obstacles along the way.

Interact Challenges
Do Three and Earn the Interact Award

Challenge (including how to "pass it forward")	Where to find the skills	What you did
Call an old friend you haven't spoken to in a while. Tell her why you miss her and hope to reconnect. Encourage her to do the same with one of her old friends.	**Page 32**	
Design your own note cards and surprise three friends with them, telling them a few of the specific qualities you enjoy about them and your friendship. Encourage your friends to pass the gesture forward.	**Pages 31–32**	
Identify a stereotype used in portraying a character on a TV show you and your friends watch. (Or think of a movie or cartoon or even a music video.) Think about who the stereotype hurts and then find a way to start a conversation with your friends about this stereotype and why you think the show is wrong to use it. Does it trouble you enough to boycott the show for a week or two—or forever? Get your friends to join in with you.	**Page 22**	
Reach out and talk with someone (at school, Girl Scouts, your place of worship) you don't usually talk with much. Ask questions and really listen to the answers. Try to clear your head of any first impressions. At the same time, make a good impression yourself by_____. Encourage your friends to do the same.	**Pages 16–21**	

Good friendship skills are all it takes to break out of the maze! Below (and on the next pages) are nine challenges.

To earn your Interact Award, simply take on three of them. But think first—the easiest path out of a maze isn't always the best one for you. Jot down what you did and how you felt about it. And remember: There's no rule that says you can't try more than three!

How did you feel about it? What did you learn?	If more people did this, how would the world be more peaceful?

More Interact Challenges

Challenge (including how to "pass it forward")	Where to find the skills	What you did
Choose a movie that features cliques, and host a viewing night with friends. Discuss how the cliques resemble (or don't) those you know at school. See if you can think of even one small thing to do to try to shift a real-life dynamic you dislike—and get your friends to do the same. (Movies to consider: "Princess Diaries," "Clueless," "Confessions of a Teenage Drama Queen," "Bratz.")	**Page 54**	
Going out (movies, mall, pizza, Girl Scout event)? Invite someone who's not normally part of your group. Ask any other friends with you to help make her feel included. Then encourage them to "pass it forward" by being the next to widen your circle.	**Page 26**	
Promise to have a "no gossip" week—for one full week, do not listen to or spread any rumors, gossip, or "mean talk." Think about making "no gossip" a way of life. Jot down when you thought of some gossip but didn't spread it. Get your friends to do the same. Encourage them to "pass it forward."	**Page 60**	
Get direct. A friend hurt your feelings. Instead of telling her (or him) directly, your urge is to vent to a few other friends. Stop the urge. Speak directly to the person who hurt your feelings. "I-statement," anyone? Encourage your friends to do the same: Get them to "pass it forward."	**Page 63**	
Create your own antibullying message and add it to the signature line of your e-mails (or add it to your voicemail or hang it in your locker or somewhere else where others can see it). Just to get your mind going, how about "Just kidding just hurts." Get your friends to "pass it forward."	**Page 74**	

How did you feel about it? What did you learn?	If more people did this, how would the world be more peaceful?

FIRST IMPRESSIONS AND STEREOTYPES

dresses   So friendly
funny
big smile   ears stick out
waaay popular   talks too much
SUPER   Too much eyeliner
JOCK   *LOUD AND PUSHY*

Most relationships start with first impressions. Did you know:

- First impressions are formed within 5 to 30 seconds of meeting someone (7 seconds is about average).

- 55 percent of first impressions are based on appearance (wardrobe, hair/makeup, body language, and facial expressions).

- 40 percent of first impressions are based on voice and speech quality (the words you choose, whether you mumble or speak clearly).

- About 5 percent of first impressions are based on *what* is said (the content of your conversation).

FINESSING FIRST IMPRESSIONS

When meeting others for the first time, what do you notice first?

Does your mind race ahead, or do you focus on the other person and what she's trying to communicate?

How do you let others know they can relax and be themselves with you?

Now, think about first impressions from the other side. What first impression do you think *you* make on people?

Do you need to change anything to make the first impression you want? If so, what?

Remember: First impressions are a two-way street. Keep that in mind when you're tempted to jump to conclusions about others!

What's Your FI IQ?

How do you think others see you? How do you see others? Test your first impressions IQ by answering these questions:

1. When people talk to you, do you act relaxed?	Y	N
2. When talking with others, do you look directly at them?	Y	N
3. Do you wait for others to finish talking before jumping in?	Y	N
4. Do you compliment others—genuinely?	Y	N
5. Do you try not to talk about yourself too much?	Y	N
6. Do you ask others for their point of view?	Y	N
7. Do you share something about yourself and try to find out something about those you're talking with?	Y	N

How'd You Do?

If you answered mostly yes, you're pretty confident about making a good first impression. You're open and welcoming to others because you let your natural self shine through and you try to find out more about those you're talking with. Use the information in this chapter to strengthen your welcoming approach when interacting with others.

If you answered no to some questions, you may not feel so comfy meeting others for the first time. You might even come off as someone you're not. Use the information in this section to improve the first impression you make. In time, you'll learn to really connect with others.

The Power of
First Impressions

Sometimes, first impressions are on target. Most of the time, they're not. Consider:

- First impressions affect how people are treated.
- Potential friendships are sometimes stopped in their tracks because of first impressions.
- Stereotypes based on first impressions often shut out new possibilities, opportunities, and adventures.
- You can't tell how a person is on the inside from what you see on the outside—but many people try to!
- First impressions can hurt—you and the other person.

Your mind often makes split-second decisions. These instinctive, spontaneous reactions often stem from our experiences, training, and knowledge—and our ingrained biases and prejudices. A gut reaction can be very useful, especially in times of danger. But when it comes to giving someone a chance, it's best to go beyond your gut.

Beneath the SURFACE

When you have some time with friends, maybe even at a sleepover, start a "deep discussion" with a "beneath the surface" question ball. Blow up an inflatable beach ball (or use an inexpensive soccer ball) and, with permanent magic marker, write some "deep" questions in each section of the ball. Then cover the questions with masking tape. Gather everyone in a circle and toss the ball to someone. Whoever gets it tears off one piece of tape and answers the question underneath. Keep the game going until everyone gets to answer a question that goes "beneath the surface."

Here are some questions to get you started. Add your own!

The last time I teased someone was

If I could be any cartoon character, it would be

The reality TV show I know I could win is

The longest I went without taking a shower is

I couldn't spend a week without

The animal sound I can make the best is

To stay healthy, I

My one vice is

I THOUGHT, YOU THOUGHT

Get together with some friends and write all your names in the "Friends" column. What was your first impression of each other? What do you think now? Were your first assumptions correct? What if you had let some first impressions get in the way of building a friendship?

Friends	First Impression	What do you think now?

You and
STEREOTYPES

Stereotypes are generalizations or assumptions that we form about people who are "members" of a particular group. They are another roadblock in the maze of relationships.

More long-lasting than first impressions, stereotypes become part of our thinking when we:

- suggest that all members of a group are the same, when, in fact, every person is different.

- allow stereotypes to be reinforced by images and attitudes on television or in cartoons, comic books, or other media.

- base our view on secondhand information.

- forget that stereotypes are usually inaccurate and full of negative assumptions, and often lead people to act in discriminating ways.

Prove that you can't judge what's inside simply by looking at the outside! Draw a circle in the middle of a plain piece of paper, with smaller circles (as many as you want) connected to and extending out from it.

Write your name in the center circle. In each of the smaller circles, write something (a characteristic or description) that makes you the person you are, such as: female, athletic, bilingual, vegetarian, religious, only child, babysitter, or anything else you consider important to who you are. Some of these may be obvious labels you or others assign to one another.

Think of and write down a stereotype associated with any of the groups you identify with that *isn't* consistent with who you are. This sentence can guide you:

I'm _____ and I'm _____.

For example, if one of your "characteristics" is "blonde," and you thought a stereotype is that blondes aren't smart, your sentence would be:

I'm *blonde* and I'm *smart*.

Share what you've written with someone you trust. Talk about a time you were especially proud to be identified with one of the characteristics you listed. Share a story about a time when you were embarrassed or afraid, or felt hurt to be identified with one of the characteristics, stereotypes, or impressions others had of you.

Time with Your Trusted Adult

Talk about first impressions and stereotypes with your trusted adult. Perhaps ask questions like:

- What was the first impression you had of me? Do you have any words of advice about this?

- Can you tell me about a time when others judged you based on stereotypes or had the wrong first impression of you? If so, how did you overcome it?

- Can you share any examples where you made decisions about relationships in your life based on first impressions and what happened as a result?

CARTOON FIT FOR A QUEEN

If anyone knows about combating global stereotypes as a way to promote world peace, it's Queen Rania of Jordan. In 2006, she hosted a black-tie dinner at the Metropolitan Museum of Art in New York to introduce network and cable executives to a Jordanian-produced cartoon TV show featuring two children—an American and an Arab. Her aim: to help children steer clear of stereotypes and prejudices with a message of trust, tolerance, and world peace. The cartoon "opens the doors to great compassion and it strengthens bonds of friendship among the children of the world," the Kuwaiti-born queen said.

For Your Peacemaker Kit

Take a few minutes to reflect on what you've uncovered on this first twist of aMAZE—the path of first impressions and stereotypes—by answering the following:

To inspire peace, I will: ....

To make a great first impression, I can:

....

To give others a chance to make a great first impression, I can:

....

Stereotyping interferes with peace in my world because:

....

Two things I can do about stereotypes—and pass on by inviting others to try doing—are:

1. ....

2. ....

1905 **Bertha Felicie Sophie von Suttner,** author of *Lay Down Your Arms* and a leader in many pacifist causes, is the first woman to be awarded the Nobel Peace Prize.

Be not disturbed at being misunderstood; be disturbed rather at not being understanding.
— *Chinese proverb*

Navigating

> *Friendship is born at that moment when one person says to another, "What! You, too? I thought I was the only one."*
>
> —*C.S. Lewis*

> **Winning has always meant much to me, but winning friends has meant the most.**
>
> —Babe Didrikson Zaharias

Sometimes it seems like we're just supposed to know how to be a good friend, without ever really thinking about what that means. So think about it: What are you really great at when it comes to making and keeping friends? What kinds of situations stretch your friendship know-how? Try this quiz to get you thinking:

1

You're psyched about sleeping over at your BFF's on Saturday. Just you, her, a new CD (which you heard was *insane*), the just-out-on-DVD movie featuring your favorite hottie, plus your favorite munchies. Then your BFF calls to say she's also invited her cousin, who just moved to town. You're kinda bummed; you were really looking forward to some quality time with your BFF! You:

a) keep silent about your feelings, but agree—in an unenthusiastic tone of voice—to still come over.

b) think of a lame excuse and cancel; you don't feel like being with someone new.

c) let your friend know that you're a bit disappointed since it's been *ages* since you've seen each other, but that you're super-excited to meet her cousin—and that she sounds really cool!

2

Elementary school is behind you and your new school has way more students than you're used to. Plus, your BFFs are in a different school. You:

a) don't see anyone you know because you keep your eyes on the ground. It takes you a while to warm up to new people.

b) keep your eye out for only the kids who seem to be popular and try to figure out a way to get in with them.

c) look for that girl you just sat next to in social studies, take a deep breath, and suggest you try to navigate the halls—and the cafeteria— together. You figure if you act confident, soon you'll actually feel it.

Friendships

3

You still haven't found a BFF in your new school, but there *are* a few girls who seem nice. In computer class, one of the girls IMs you about meeting after school today. At the same time, your old BFF texts you from her new school to say she's bored and wants to see if you can chat after school. You:

a) ignore both; you just want to be alone—relationships take too much energy!

b) blow off your new friend and spend that time gossiping with your old BFF.

c) quickly text your old BFF that you can't wait to hear what's going on and would love to chat tonight at home. IM the new girl that you'd love to link up after school.

4

Your family has just moved, so you're the new girl in school. You feel *so* out of your element! When that girl from your homeroom who dresses kind of uniquely sees you struggling to open your locker and offers to help, what do you do?

a) Give her clothes an up-and-down look and tell her no thanks, you're fine on your own.

b) Look down the hall to see if anyone from the cool crowd is watching before answering.

c) Accept her offer immediately. You're so glad to have someone to talk to—plus she seems really nice and made a funny comment in homeroom today.

5

It's last period and you're really anxious to go home. Plus, you're not loving the clothes you're wearing today. After school is the annual fair to find out all about the teams and clubs you could join. You:

a) skip it. You're so tired and just want to veg in front of the TV.

b) stick around but act like you are above joining any of these clubs—cool kids don't, right?

c) go! You think you would be good at soccer and have always been into photography, so you could sign up for both.

6

You have plans with friends for the weekend—and you're really looking forward to it. Then some girls in the more popular crowd invite you to go to the mall with them. What do you do?

a) Decide that it would be easier not to do anything with anybody!

b) Brag to the girls you were going to hang with about how the popular clique wants you to come along. You can't believe it!

c) Tell the "popular" kids you're really not into the mall and have plans that day. But you suggest that maybe you all can hang out some other time. You'd really like them to get to know your other friends!

In science class, the teacher asks everyone to get into small groups for a project. You:

a) right away form a group with your two best friends.

b) grab the smartest kid in the class and say you want to be in her group.

c) ask the boy you saw reading your favorite book on the bus if he wants to work together.

The new girl in class seems to have taken a liking to you. She seems OK and your moms work together, but you haven't spent any real time with her. On the bus to school one day, she whispers to you who she's crushing on—and swears you to secrecy. You:

a) run and tell the secret to the "It Chick" in school. You are sort of friendly with her. This juicy tidbit will give you a reason to get some time with her—maybe bond a little over it!

b) tell the guy. He's super-cute and maybe he and his friend and you and your friend can eat together in the cafeteria.

c) tell her you won't tell anyone—and mean it.

You're shopping with your mom and run into another girl from school with her mom. The moms get to talking and soon you're all having coffee and dessert together. You:

a) keep pretty quiet; you're feeling pretty antisocial today.

b) talk about yourself—you've been told you've got a great gift for gab.

c) try to think of something fun to talk about and ask her questions while you share stories about your life, too. You might have something in common.

Depending on your answers to the quiz, check out these tips for new ways to navigate friendships:

Got A's?

It's OK to take some quiet time for yourself along this big maze of life. It can be energizing. But you may need to push yourself a little to reach out and enjoy the company of others—and not just the same old others! The more you connect and interact, the more your circles of belonging will energize you. And remember, to get good friends you may need to open up—your heart *and* your mouth.

Bounded by B's?

Are you sometimes more worried about how your friendships look to others than actually enjoying the people who cross your path? Don't be so wanting to be the center of attention that you miss some of what you might enjoy around you.

Seeing C's?

You're showing great relationship skills. Use your strengths to bring some "A's" and "B's" along.

Alphabet Soup?

If you've got a little of all the letters going on, that's normal! Nobody is one way all the time. Relationships let you try a new approach every day. When you shift, people around you may find they need to shift a little, too. So stop and think about your friendships—where are they landing you on the happiness scale? What might you want to do differently? And take heart—there will always be a next time!

Human relationships, like life itself, can never remain static.

— Eleanor Roosevelt

What other girls say about friendship:

I love that I can trust my friends—trust is very important to me, and once someone breaks my trust, it is very difficult for me to see them in the same light and be "normal" with them again.
— **Bianca, 17, New Jersey**

It's important that friends have a sense of humor, and it's important that they care about me. — **Alissa, 16, New York**

My friends accept me for who I am. They know all my good and bad qualities, and they still like me. They stand beside me and help me through tough times. They make me laugh and appreciate life more.
— **Ciara, 15, California**

The best quality in a friend is loyalty. Your friends will always be tight with you and will never leave you just to chill with other people. They can be trusted with your deepest, darkest secrets.
— **Vicki, 13, Pennsylvania**

What Really Matters

We all know what we look for in a friend, but sometimes what we think we want and what we actually seek out are two very different things. Be honest with yourself as you go down the following list and prioritize each quality. Place a 1 next to the most important attribute and a 13 next to the least. If the qualities you think are important aren't listed, add them in and rank them, too.

_____ Appearance (how she looks)

_____ Intelligence (how smart she is)

_____ Affluence (how much money she has)

_____ Attitude (her outlook on life)

_____ Spiritual beliefs

_____ Race/ethnicity/family background

_____ Popularity (how many friends she has and/or if she has the "right" friends)

_____ Loyalty (if she is trustworthy and dependable)

_____ Honesty (if she tells the truth)

_____ Fun to be with

_____ Understands me

_____ Neighborhood where she lives _____

_____ Something else you think is important: _____

Did any of your rankings surprise you? Is there anything you want to change? How could you start making some changes—even small ones—to bring your actions closer to what really matters to you?

Now, look at the list below. How many of these qualities do you look for in a friend? How many of them do *you* offer to *your friends?*

Qualities of Friends

Loyal Dependable **Assertive** Makes others feel good about themselves **Honest** Understanding **Confident** Nice/kind **Powerful** Good listener **Good mediator** Sense of humor **Popular** Easygoing **Wears the right clothes** Fun-loving **Patient** Flexible **Good at a lot of stuff** Good communicator **Optimistic** Trustworthy **Shares similar interests** Helpful **Accepts people for who they are** Gives good advice **Generous** Independent **Keeps a secret** Tells me what to do **Caring** Spontaneous **Respectful** Similar religious beliefs **Sensitive to my feelings** Athletic **Thoughtful** Attractive **Shares** Stands by me **Cool** Flatters me **Courageous** Inspiring **Knows a lot of people** Creative **Open-minded** Intelligent **Tries to make people be their best** Likes to have me around **Values diversity** Good leader **Makes me look good**

Profile, Please!

Now that you've thought about what you look for in a friend, turn the lens on yourself. What kind of a friend are *you*? What kind of friend do you want to be?

Create a friendship profile. Include attributes you're proud of ("I'm a great listener") and those you may not be proud of ("I sometimes have trouble keeping a really juicy secret to myself").

Then create a list of your Top 10 tips for keeping friendships going strong. With your friends, take these tips and post them at home, at school, at a Girl Scout event—wherever you think they might be useful to others.

My Friendship Profile

I'm really proud of ....

One thing I'm not so great at is ....

The quality that I really want in a friend is ....

The one thing a friend of mine should never do is ....

I'm a terrific person to have as a friend because I ....

My hit single about friendship would be called ....

One thing I am trying to do more of in my friendships is ....

One thing I am trying to do less of in my friendships is ....

One thing I would never do to a friend is ....

The best thing a friend has ever done for me is ....

Top 10 Great Friendship Tips

1.   6.
2.   7.
3.   8.
4.   9.
5.   10.

FRIENDS FOREVER

Think about two sets of really good friends you either know or know about. (Maybe these friendships are between your mother and a friend, TV or film friends, you and a friend, or any other friend combination you know.) Why do you think these friendships are great? What do the friends seem to do to keep the friendships going?

How about famous friendships? Other than the ones featured below, who else can you think of? Based on what you know about famous friends (which might not be the truth!), which friendships seem pretty healthy? Which seem not so healthy? Why?

FAMOUS FRIENDSHIPS

Nicole Kidman and Naomi Watts

Penélope Cruz and Salma Hayek

Jennifer Aniston and Courteney Cox

Hilary Duff and Hayden Panettiere

Beyoncé Knowles and Kelly Rowland

Oprah Winfrey and Gayle King

Drew Barrymore and Cameron Diaz

FICTIONAL BFFS

Lucy and Ethel
(*I Love Lucy*)

Mary and Rhoda
(*The Mary Tyler Moore Show*)

Laverne and Shirley
(*Laverne & Shirley*)

Carly and Sam
(*iCarly*)

Betty and Veronica
(Archie Comics)

Wilma and Betty
(*The Flintstones*)

Anne Shirley and Diana Barry
(*Anne of Green Gables*)

10 Snack FRIENDS

Got the munchies? Consider these terrific snack duos:

Peanut butter on apple slices (almond butter's nice, too!)

Carrots and yogurt dip

Almonds and raisins

Dark chocolate and raspberries

Brown bread toast with jam

Cereal with bananas

Pretzels with mustard

Popcorn with a sprinkle of parmesan cheese

Baked chips and guacamole

A bowl of red and green grapes

And, to drink, ice cold water with fruit slices floating in it!

WHAT'S YOUR FaVORITE "MOSTLY GOOD FOR YOU" Snack?

....

....

Next time you're with friends, swap some snack tips. Better yet, take turns supplying the snacks! Be sure to ask about allergies before you serve anything.

say cheese!

Invite your friends to a photo-booth session to get your pictures taken together. Or use your own camera and take turns being the photog. Make silly faces, hug, cut loose!

Paste the photos (or others of your friends) in the frames below. Then, below each picture, list the qualities each has that you value.

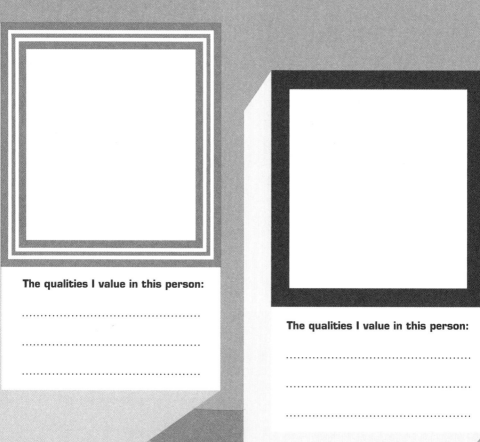

The qualities I value in this person:

....

....

....

The qualities I value in this person:

....

....

....

The qualities I value in this person:

....

....

....

A Song Worth Singing

"Make new friends,
but keep the old;
one is silver
and the other is gold."

This Girl Scout song is
simple—but pretty amazing
when sung in rounds in a
circle of friends!

The qualities I value in this person:

....

....

....

TRUST

When you talk to a friend about the friendship you share, lots of opinions, ideas, and feelings are bound to come up. That's a good thing. To feel safe about sharing with others, set some guidelines you both can agree to. Here are some sample "rules" to get you started:

- **This conversation is between us; no gossiping afterward!**
- **Let's remember that we both care about each other.**
- **No silent treatment.**

Get Legal (just kidding): Friendship Bill of Rights

Now that you know what kind of friend you want, and the kind of friend you want to be, why not turn those "wants" into an action plan. Create a Friendship Bill of Rights that spells out your rights and responsibilities in your friendships. Figure out:

- what actions a friend may take that justify ending your friendship
- what types of situations require going to a trusted adult for help
- what other information should be included

Sign the document to represent your commitment to the values included in the bill. Place your Bill of Rights where it will be most useful as a reminder of your dedication to your friends (on your computer monitor, as wallpaper on your cell phone, inside your locker door).

For Your Peacemaker Kit

Why are true friends one of the most remarkable treasures human beings have?

. . . .

What is one quality or skill you are going to try to use more often in your friendships?

. . . .

What is one idea you can suggest to help other people improve their friendships?

. . . .

How could one or two of the ideas you had in this section of aMAZE create more peace in your world?

. . . .

1931 After a lifetime of advocacy for women's rights, racial equality, labor reform, social justice, and pacifism, **Jane Addams** is awarded the Nobel Peace Prize. She's the first American woman to receive it.

friendship obstacles

Ever feel pressured to do one thing when your gut (which is usually in tune with your values) tells you to do another? That's a pretty common obstacle in the maze of friendships. In fact, you'll probably encounter it in one form or another all your life.

Do this. Don't do that. Fit in. Stand out. Be different. Not so different. Be strong. Not too strong. Get good grades. Why are you carrying all your books around? You've got a flair for style. You're wearing that?!

So take a stand—right now! Pressure isn't just what others do to you. It's also what you might be doing to others. Build up your courage! Make decisions that represent your true self and maybe even inspire others to do the same.

under pressure

Peer pressure can be negative or positive. It can also be silent. Here's an example of silent peer pressure from Melinda, who's 15:

Once when we had a substitute teacher, a couple of the class clowns pranked her by screeching "oy" every time her back was turned. It got really annoying after a while, and the teacher got very upset, but no one told her who was doing it. Telling on a classmate is pretty much social suicide.

Are there rules about where to sit at lunchtime or on the bus? About the kinds of clothing that are "in"? These are also examples of "silent" peer pressure. Can you think of others?

have you ever . . .

- changed your appearance or clothing style to please others?

- done something wrong because you thought it would make you fit in (shoplifting, drinking, smoking . . .)?

- not done something you really wanted to do because kids you want to be friends with weren't doing it?

- pushed your friend to do something she really did not feel comfortable doing?

- made fun of someone who said "no" to something everyone else was doing?

- gone along with the crowd to the mall or the movies even though there were other activities you really would have enjoyed more?

- decided something was "too corny" for you because you saw other kids rolling their eyes, even though you thought it was nice?

- given away answers to a test or a tough homework assignment just to please other kids? (That's different from teaching someone something they don't know!)

- done something against important beliefs of your family?

- silently gone along with something that you knew was just mean?

- dropped friends because other "friends" didn't like them—even though you really did?

- done something else you think was a form of peer pressure?

Where Do You Stand?

Be careful of your thoughts, for your thoughts become your words;
Be careful of your words, for your words become your deeds;
Be careful of your deeds, for your deeds become your habits;
Be careful of your habits, for your habits become your character;
Be careful of your character, for your character becomes your destiny.

— Author unknown

saying "no" to pressure

Everyone wants that powerful feeling of belonging. Being connected to others is an affirmation that we are worthy, we matter. And that's a human need! Sometimes we want that belonging so badly that we think a small trade-off of some of our values won't matter. But small trade-offs add up, chipping away at our sense of what is right. When that sense becomes blurry, you may find yourself caving in to peer pressure more and more.

Giving in to pressure—or dishing it out—comes from a lack of self-confidence. If you say no, will people still like you? The right people will! Being confident means choosing your own path—one that, in the end, feels really great and is lined with true friends.

It's naive to believe that you won't care at all what other people think of you. But caring too much certainly won't make you feel good. So listen to your inner voice. You'll be happier, even if it means not being accepted right now by some people. Here are a few suggestions for how to cope when you feel pressured:

Imagine how you will feel afterward. What will it cost you to go along with the others, as opposed to staying true to yourself? This may be all it takes for you to say "no thanks" with confidence.

Share your feelings with others in the group. Many of them may be feeling the same things but are too scared to say so. Don't aim to change their view; help them understand yours.

Recognize you can't have it both ways. Perhaps you don't completely give in to peer pressure, but you also don't express your true feelings. Then you're leading a double life—one in front of your friends, another when you're on your own. The guilt can build up. Speak up or get some new friends.

Use humor. Making light of a situation ("I don't mind being president of the loser-of-the-month club") might just take the pressure off without making you look like a "goody-two-shoes."

Ask your parents if you can "blame them." Everyone can relate to fearing the trouble you might get into if your parents find out you've done something they disapprove of. (Your parents probably won't mind if you use them as an excuse to do the right thing!)

Pick your friends wisely. The best friends are ones who share your values and like you for who you are. If you're often pressured to go against your beliefs—or you pressure others—you may be hanging with the wrong crowd. It could be time to make some new friends.

Get involved in something new. If your relationships constantly involve drama-rama related to giving and getting pressure, expand your world! Join a club, take up dancing, start a babysitting business, try out for the track team. Do something that breaks your routine and the pressures that go with it.

Celebrate your differences. Too much "same" in relationships can be just too-too matchy-matchy—like a clothing style on overdrive. Whoever invented cool stuff like the iPod was probably not following a crowd! So jot down some of your quirks—things you like about yourself. Write them in a really positive and affirming way. Read them and add to them whenever you need a confidence boost! Here's an example to get you started: "I am really good at organizing games so that little kids have fun. I like spending time doing this. I am going to enjoy my decision to be me!"

Defy the Pressure

Imagine you write an advice column and have received the following questions from girls seeking your advice. Answer their questions and explain why you're giving this particular advice.

The most popular boy in 7th grade asked me to the movies. I've never been on a date because my parents want me to wait until I'm 15. The theater is at the mall, so I could ask my mom to drop me off as if I'm meeting friends, and then meet him at the movies. What should I do?

— Guyless Mall Rat

Dear Mall Rat,

....

....

....

....

I've been selected to the all-city under-13 basketball squad. It's a real honor. Problem is, I got picked because they mixed me up with another girl with the same name. She's the sister of a star player, and I've been told she was the one who was supposed to be chosen. I haven't told my parents or the coach the truth. Since I'm better than she is and it shows, my friends on the squad are urging me to stay quiet. What should I do?

— Mixed-up Hoopster

Dear Hoopster,

....

....

....

My closest friends are in marching band. We bonded because we always go on band trips together and have a blast playing cards and pulling practical jokes on each other on the long bus rides. Over the summer, I took dance lessons and found I'm pretty good, so I tried out for cheerleading and made it! Now I'd like to drop out of band and do cheerleading. But if I drop out, I'll probably lose all my band pals because we'll no longer share the same memories and inside jokes, and they think cheerleaders are lame. What should I do?

— Cheerleader in a Band Uniform

Dear Cheerleader,

....
....
....
....

Make up your own dilemma and then write the advice to go with it.

....
....
....
....
....
....
....
....
....
....
....
....

Oh Boy!

You know the deal: Two girls have a groovy, long-term friendship and along comes a boy. Suddenly everything changes. Maybe both girls are crushing on the same boy or one girl has been spending a lot more time with her boyfriend than with her friend. Arguments flare. Someone feels hurt, confused, betrayed.

Lauren's example of boy trouble: "Jasmine bailed on our plans to get manicures together because her crush asked her to go to a basketball game. I tried to understand because I knew it was important to her. But when she ditched me two more times in a row to be with him, I was really hurt. It was as if he was suddenly more important to her than I was—and we've been best friends since second grade!"

When Lauren talked to Jasmine about how she was feeling, Jasmine realized she needed to make sure she didn't neglect her best friend just because she has a guy in her life. Jasmine balanced her schedule and now has enough time for her best gal and her guy.

How's Your Balancing Act?

How well are you balancing *your* time among various friends, family, and your boyfriend? If they're important to you, they all deserve some quality time. Use colored markers to fill in the chart below. Assign each friend (and your guy) a color, and create a key at the bottom to show which color represents which person. Then, for each day of the week, color in the amount of time you spend with that person. Include phone, IM, text, and face-to-face time. At the end of the week, evaluate your chart. If necessary, balance your time better. Your friends—and your guy—will respect you for your thoughtful balancing act!

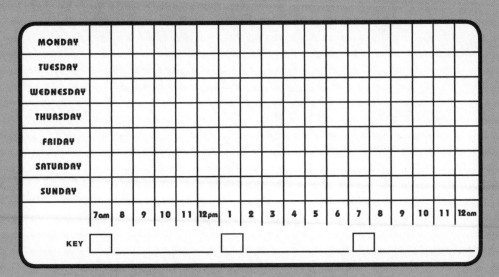

	7am	8	9	10	11	12pm	1	2	3	4	5	6	7	8	9	10	11	12am
MONDAY																		
TUESDAY																		
WEDNESDAY																		
THURSDAY																		
FRIDAY																		
SATURDAY																		
SUNDAY																		

KEY ☐ _____ ☐ _____ ☐ _____

IS YOUR JEALOUSY SHOWING?

There will be times when you wish more than anything for something a friend of yours has. That's jealousy. When that Green-Eyed Monster shows up, a whole bunch of emotions can get tangled up inside you and you just feel weird. It's important to recognize these feelings, and it's totally OK to have them.

But it's not OK to lash out at, gossip about, or in any way abuse your friend because of your feelings. It's up to you (and those in whom you confide) to channel your energy elsewhere. Otherwise, your jealousy can poison your thoughts and make you do things you may later regret.

So, the question is: How do you deal with jealousy? Work through it by focusing on what's really important, like what *you have*—not just your material possessions but your great personal qualities.

Say, for example, you're jealous that your friend has a whole new social life going on because she joined the drama club. Drama might not be your thing, so take some time to find *your* thing. Imagine how much new stuff you'll be able to share with your friend when you talk.

Here are some situations that could make you feel jealous. Brainstorm some solutions with someone you trust.

1. You have a crush on a guy but don't know how to approach him. Now you see him walking hand in hand with another girl.

   ....

2. You set your sights on improving your grade in your least favorite subject. It means extra studying, but you put in the time. Your efforts pay off—you get a significantly improved grade on your report card. But your best friend does even better, and she hardly studied.

   ....

3. You have your heart set on becoming the editor of the school literary magazine. But the faculty adviser chooses another student for that job.

   ....

4. You wear a totally cute new outfit on the first day of school. But another girl in your homeroom is wearing it, too! Even worse—she's getting all the attention.

   ....

Time with Your Trusted Adult

Friendships are wonderful and difficult—often at the same time! Ask your trusted adult whether she's ever had a conflict with a friend.

How did she try to resolve it?

....

What friendship qualities is she most proud of?

....

Has she ever had to end an unhealthy relationship?

....

Create Your Own
No-Pressure Zone

Make a Top 10 list for how to best deal with peer pressure. Maybe even make it into a bookmark and pass it on.

10 Great Tips for Dealing with Peer Pressure

1. ....

2. ....

3. ....

4. ....

5. ....

6. ....

7. ....

8. ....

9. ....

10. ....

Who's on Your Make Peace List?

Imagine you were just chosen to board the next space shuttle to try life on another planet. You may not return for decades. But you have a chance to make peace with three people on Earth before you leave. Who would you call and what would you say?

. . . .

. . . .

. . . .

What are you waiting for? Start dialing!

For Your Peacemaker Kit

I can resolve conflict by:

What values of the Girl Scout Law do I hold dear?
How will I show I live these values—no matter what?

....

What are two things I can always have ready to say when someone wants me to do something that I don't want to do?

....

What are some activities I'm involved in, or that I can get involved in, where I can be myself—no matter what?

....

Have I been pressuring my friends to do anything they don't want to do?
If yes, I will

....

If I can recognize I am feeling jealous, I will try to work past it by

....

What are two relationship strategies you thought about in this section of aMAZE that you think would create more peace in your world—if you use them and encourage others to use them too?

....

....

1946 **Emily Greene Balch** wins the Nobel Peace Prize for her work with the Women's International League for Peace and Freedom, the world's oldest women's peace organization. The league's aim is "to work for permanent peace" worldwide.

52

Friendships the World Over: A Girl Scout Legacy

Juliette Gordon Low, the founder of Girl Scouts, truly believed in having friends around the world. When she began Girl Scouts, she envisioned it being "for the girls of Savannah, and all America, and all the world."

Of Chimps and Changes

Jane Goodall sat alone for months in the jungle habitat of wild chimpanzees, waiting for them to become comfortable with her presence. This enabled her to observe them not only using tools but making them—a revolutionary discovery.

What revolutionary changes might the world experience if leaders took the same time and care building relationships—across geographical, racial, and cultural borders?

Cliques and Conflicts

Truly belonging to a supportive social circle is one of life's greatest joys. It's a powerful feeling to be accepted by peers who recognize your best qualities, accept your flaws (well, your one flaw anyway!), and encourage you to reach for your dreams.

How do you achieve this magical circle of belonging? You create it through your interactions and then you work to keep it healthy and growing. But as you head toward that nurturing circle, other dynamics may draw you in. After all, conflict-free relationships don't just happen. So grab your compass and keep navigating this maze!

What's a Clique?

Have you ever been part of a group where you feel judged and controlled? Or have you been part of a group that morphs from a supportive crowd into one that restricts your social landscape and requires you to be someone you're not? When that happens, you've landed in a clique.

Cliques have lots of rules, and they often deliberately include or exclude members. Most of the time, they create a hostile environment for everyone around.

> *Whenever you're in conflict with someone, there is one factor that can make the difference between damaging your relationship and deepening it. That factor is attitude.*
> — **William James**

Here's Sharina's example of a clique. "There is a group of girls at my school who always act like they're better than everyone. They have these rules, like they sit at a special table in the back of the cafeteria and no one else is allowed to sit there. They all carry designer bags. They only hang out with the rich kids or the super-smart kids. They're not usually mean . . . but they never let other girls into the group."

For their members, cliques provide:

☆ a sense of belonging (even though it's false).

☆ protection from other groups.

☆ a self-esteem boost (though only temporary: I must be OK if I belong).

But cliques also:

☆ keep people out.

☆ think anyone not in the clique is a loser.

☆ demand members follow "rules."

☆ cause people to lose their individuality.

In a clique, power is uneven. Some girls have lots of it; others give up their personal power—even the power to voice their opinions—in order to belong.

Think you're part of a clique? An "attitude check" may be in order:

☆ Does your group easily include others and value individuality?

☆ Does your circle expand and grow?

These are important ways to keep your world a welcoming place.

Are You in a *Clique?*

Even if your circle of friends isn't officially a clique, it may act like one. Test it out:

When's the last time someone new came into your circle?

Take a look around: Are you all "the same"?

Do one or a few girls frequently make all the decisions?

Do some girls follow others, no matter what?

Do you ever feel caught between your values and your attachment to the group?

Does the group keep you in just to pick on you—or just for access to something you have?

Are you truly accepted as part of the group, or are you just watching from the sidelines?

Based on the clique characteristics you've just read about, list all the groups and activities you take part in—formal ones like sports teams and extracurricular clubs, and informal ones like your lunch table and the school bus. Now decide: Are they "circles" or "cliques"? Why? Do you want to make any changes?

Group/Activity	Is it a clique?	Why or why not?	What does belonging do for you?	Thoughts about staying/going/ changing it up?

Your GS Group: Clique or Friendly Circle?

Would you describe your GS Cadette group as a clique or a circle of friends? Have you thought about how new people feel when they join? How is power distributed in the group? Does each girl get to voice her opinion, or is the group controlled by a select few? Does the group include others, value individuality, promote respect? If not, how are you living up to the Girl Scout Law? When your GS group goes to events with other GS groups, are you excited to reach out and make new friends or do you stick within your group? Anything you want to change?

How to Achieve
Clique Control

It may seem impossible at times, but there are many ways to make non-clique friends and have fun!

1. **Mix and mingle.** Whether you live in a big city, a small town, or anywhere in between, there are plenty of places to meet interesting people. Just interact with everyone you meet, whether on your sports teams, volunteer work, social activities, or in class.

2. **Don't let cliques eat up your time.** Remember: You have a family waiting to spend time with you, too.

3. **Choose friends who share common interests and don't think the highest priority in their day is putting others down.** Don't just hang with people because they are considered part of the popular crowd.

4. **Open your eyes and your mind.** You'll find fabulous people all around you— of all ages and backgrounds. So be a leader—expand your network. Being inclusive is what popularity is all about.

5. **Stand up for yourself and others.** Don't let friends treat you the wrong way or put you down. Take the lead in discussions and social planning. Deal with conflict, rumors, or gossip within the group head-on.

Remember, no one can make you feel inferior without your consent.

— Eleanor Roosevelt

Test Your Gut!

Fill in the blanks with what comes to mind first:

1. When I see a girl being excluded by other girls, I ....

....

2. When I want to make new friends, I ....

....

3. If I'm seen as being mean or snarky toward other girls, I immediately ....

....

4. The best way to break up with a friend or get out of a clique in a
peaceful way is ....

....

5. Five ways to let others know you value their friendship are ....

....

....

6. Share your gut reactions and invite others to do the same!

....

....

Gossip! Sometimes it seems there's no escape from it, right? It's a powerful force that can destroy relationships that have taken years to build. It's just not worth it. But what's a girl to do? Well, not starting it—and not repeating it—is a great place to begin. As a leader with character, you can certainly find many other things to talk about!

Tracking the Gossip

Think of a time when gossip made its way through your circle of friends. Fill in the flow chart below to track the path of the gossip and the situation that resulted from it.

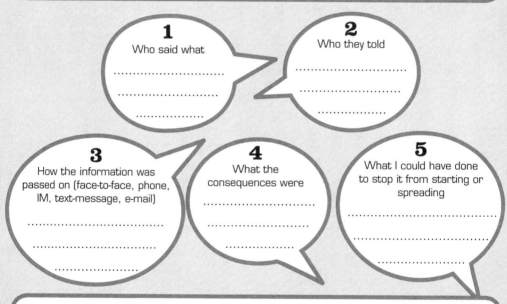

1 Who said what
....
....
....

2 Who they told
....
....
....

3 How the information was passed on (face-to-face, phone, IM, text-message, e-mail)
....
....
....

4 What the consequences were
....
....
....

5 What I could have done to stop it from starting or spreading
....
....
....

Some parts of the chart may be tough to fill in—like where the gossip originated or exactly what the consequences were. That makes total sense, because part of what is so destructive about gossip is that it's hard to track. So what can you do? Team with your friends and agree to keep gossip to a minimum, using some of the ideas given in the next activity.

Healing Old Wounds

"Sticks and stones may break my bones but words can never hurt me" is an old children's saying. Actually, words can hurt—a lot. Gossip is one of the main ways in which words can be used as weapons. Have you ever gotten burned by gossip?

Are you guilty of gossiping? Either way, you've got some healing to do.

Daria's example of gossip: "My friend Jillian bragged that she got a higher score than me in the fencing finals and was better than me. To get back at her, I spilled her secret that her twin brother, Jeff, was arrested for shoplifting. When Jeff found out that so many people knew, he got really depressed and stopped coming to school. He also got into a major fight with Jillian and didn't speak to her for months. I hurt Jeff and damaged his relationship with Jillian by blabbing a secret instead of just talking to Jillian about how I was feeling. Now Jillian will never trust me again."

Write your own **"The Gossip Ends Here"** pledge, sign it, and post it where you can see it everyday. When gossip comes your way, tell the gossip-passer about your pledge and why you refuse to pass it on. You can even attach your pledge to gossipy e-mails, or add a shortened version to text messages. Your anti-gossiping stand will get around!

THE GOSSIP ENDS HERE

I pledge never to pass on gossip because

. . . .

Gossip is . . . . **and** . . . .

and I don't do it.

Join me in putting an end to gossip.

Signed,

. . . .

Your Name   **Date**

CONFLICT RESOLUTION:

I CAN DO IT!

Talking about friendship dramas can be tough. But when conflicts arise—from gossip, cliques, or other friendship issues—it's always best to talk about them.

The problem is that when people are upset, they tend to speak in "you-statements" ("You're a liar!" or "You are so stupid"). "You-statements" immediately put the other person on the defensive. She'll feel attacked and will likely toss some "you-statements" right back at you. Then the conflict might escalate and you'll miss the opportunity to help each other understand what's wrong and how you might fix it.

So instead of a "you-statement," offer an "I-statement." Focus on one specific behavior or action of the other person and how it affected you.

An "I-statement" ("I feel hurt" or "I feel sad") lets you communicate your feelings in a strong way because you're making it about you, not the other person, and your feelings are communicated openly and honestly. It allows the other person to really hear you—without feeling threatened. Check out this formula for expressing yourself with "I-statements":

I feel . . . .
(say your feeling)

when you . . . .
(describe one specific action)

because . . . .
(say why the action connects to your feeling)

When Using "I-Statements,"

1

If you and your friend have had lots of good times in the past, don't be quick to throw away all those good memories or the possibility of future fun together.

2

Keep separate incidents separate. If you lump together every wrong thing you feel someone has ever done to you and start ranting, you won't leave much room for your friend to try to adjust a behavior that is hurtful.

3

There are two sides to every story. Communicate openly with each other about the situation and don't listen to gossip and rumors.

Keep These Pointers in Mind:

4

Be honest—with yourself and each other. Your friend might not be perfect, but are you?

5

Using "I-statements" takes practice. When you start using them, your friends might be a little thrown off course at first. Don't give up. They really work! Pass this strategy on to your friends—so you can support one another in using them.

Now, try this with a friend: Choose one of the scenarios below and role-play the conflict and see where it goes. Then try role-playing it again, using "I-statements." Repeat the process with a second scenario, letting the other person go first. Afterward, discuss which kind of messaging works best for communicating feelings and resolving conflicts.

SITUATION

TYPICAL "YOU" MESSAGE

POSSIBLE "I-STATEMENT" RESPONSE

Over the past month, your best friend has been distant. You know she's busy with school and her part-time job, but every time you chat with her, she talks about her problems and then rushes you off the phone when you begin to talk about your day.

You are so selfish. You are not the only one who's busy and who has a lot going on! You know I have a dance competition coming up and have been practicing three hours a day with my group to get the routines right!

When you rush me off the phone when I have problems, I feel hurt and unsupported. When can you make time for me?

You have a morning class with one friend and then meet up with everyone in your group for lunch. Lately, when you and your friend are together in class, she always agrees with what you say. But when you're in your full group, she says things to put you down. The rest of the group is oblivious since they're not with you in the morning.

Why are you being so two-faced?! You're not impressing anyone by being a hypocrite!

When you publicly criticized me at lunch, I felt confused about our friendship. You agree with me on almost everything when we're hanging out alone. Can we talk about this?

SURPRISED UNCOMFORTABLE SAD HELPLESS DISMAYED

SITUATION

TYPICAL "YOU" MESSAGE

POSSIBLE "I-STATEMENT" RESPONSE

Nearly every day, your friend mentions how expensive her outfit is and how her mom keeps buying her new clothes for the season. Your parents think it's silly to spend so much on clothes you'll grow out of in a year. You do, too, but you're still dying for some new designer jeans.

Why do you constantly brag about your clothes? You are not better or smarter just because you wear cool designer clothes every day!

Write your own "I-statement:"

When you . . . .

I feel . . . .

. . . . *!*

You hear your best friend ask your boyfriend to help her with her homework on Friday afternoon, although you and he have a standing date every week to do just that.

I can't believe you would ask my boyfriend to help you with homework! You know he helps me with homework on Friday afternoons. Are you trying to steal him from me?

Write your own "I-statement:"

When you . . . .

I feel . . . .

. . . . *!*

Your soccer buddy teases you in front of the team about missing a goal. When you try to defend yourself, she calls you a "wuss" for not being able to take a joke.

You are always mean to me. You are such a horrible friend!

Write your own "I-statement:"

When you . . . .

I feel . . . .

. . . . *!*

GUILTY HURT LONELY MISERABLE REJECTED

Strategies for Conflict Resolution

Now that you've got a handle on "I-statements," look over these Strategies for Conflict Resolution.

TALK IT OUT

Choose a place where you and your friend can sit down and talk about the problem without distractions, and set a time to get together. Use "I-statements" when you talk. Encourage the other person to do the same. Commit to hearing and listening with the intention of coming to peace.

SHIFT THE POV

Try seeing the conflict from the other person's point of view (POV). Ask the person to do the same for you. Remember, the truth can hurt—but seeing the situation from each other's perspective gives you both a chance to grow.

SAY "SORRY" AND MEAN IT

Acknowledge your mistakes; also accept a friend's apology.

BUILD TRUST

Use your creativity to figure out how to trust each other again.

COMPROMISE

Sometimes you have to give a little to get a little.

PUT IT OFF

Sometimes you need to give a conflict some rest. Walk away and give it some time.

LET IT GO

Some conflicts just aren't worth it. Let it go—for real. But if you can't—if it's going to sit and boil in your gut—try another strategy!

SOLVE THE PROBLEM

Sometimes it's possible to find a solution and end the conflict.

SEEK HELP

Some conflicts call for third-party intervention. Talk to an adult you trust.

Now think about two friendship conflicts you're facing in your life. Which strategy do you think would be best to try out on each of your conflicts?

Fill in the conflict log, making entries for each conflict in your life, the strategy you'd like to take, and the results. If you see that one strategy isn't working, try another. Develop a color-coding system and use it to label each entry—for example: red for "boiling point"; black for "stuck"; green for "get help"; blue for "solved." Track the progress of each conflict: Is it escalating (getting worse) or de-escalating (getting better)?

Conflict	Strategy	Results

WHEN IT'S TIME TO LET GO

There may be times, after a fight or round of gossip, when you think a friendship isn't worth it. Sometimes it really is time for a breakup. When you have a quiet moment, ask yourself: Does your friend frequently . . .

- urge you to do things that are not safe or are wrong?

- try to control who you see, talk to, or hang out with?

- gossip or spread rumors about you (as a repeat pattern)?

- make you feel bad about yourself?

If you answered yes to any of these, it may be time to reassess your friendship. Speak with someone you trust about the best way to move on.

SILENT TREATMENT IS NO TREAT

Sticks and stones are hard on bones
Aimed with angry art,
Words can sting like anything
But silence breaks the heart.
— Suzanne Nichols

One of the most harmful and hurtful ways to express anger to a friend or family member is by refusing to talk to them. The other person never has a chance to learn what's wrong and fix it. So, even if you need a cooling-off period, try to talk out the issue once you're more up for it. And remember: Sometimes friends understand you; sometimes they don't. When a best friend really doesn't understand, be patient. There's probably a shortfall of your own that you'd like her to be patient with.

For Your Peacemaker Kit

Think up a little saying—a friendly reminder like "Keep breathing," "No blame," "Life is too short," or "All will be well"—any soothing words that you can repeat to yourself whenever friendship drama-rama flares up. Call it your friendship mantra if you like. Encourage others to do the same.

Life is too short!

....

....

....

....

....

1976 The efforts of **Betty Williams** and **Mairead Corrigan**, cofounders of Women for Peace (later the Community for Peace People), lead to a 70 percent drop in the violence in Northern Ireland—and the Nobel Peace Prize.

Time with Your Trusted Adult

At some point, all of us have to deal with group politics and cliques. Ask your trusted adult how she tries to create inclusive circles of belonging in her life. What have been the hardest "clique situations" for her, and what lessons can she pass on to you?

....

....

....

....

....

....

....

....

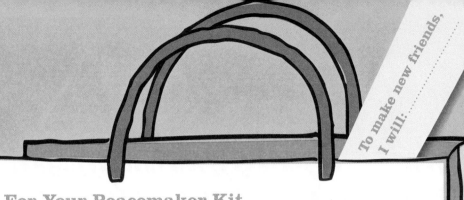

To make new friends, I will: ....

For Your Peacemaker Kit

You likely have a very different perspective when you're standing in the middle of a clique—or in the middle of a conflict—compared to when you're on the sidelines. So get out of the middle and think about how you can be a leader who builds connections among different groups.

Answer "true" or "false" to the following statements. Then think about related actions you can take to create more peace in your world.

The activities I'm involved in build bridges among diverse groups at school or within Girl Scouts.	T	F
Each of my friends brings something special to our relationship, and my friends would say the same of me.	T	F
I am a leader when it comes to making others, especially those who are misunderstood, feel more accepted and valued.	T	F
If I see cliques doing something that goes against the qualities of friendship I value, or if I'm part of a clique that does something contradicting my friendship values, I can express my feelings openly.	T	F
My circle of friends shares our personal power evenly. Everyone gets a chance to drive our discussions and decisions, social and otherwise.	T	F

Two things I can do related to this passageway in the maze that would bring more peace to my world are:

1. ....

2. ....

1991 **Aung San Suu Kyi** receives the Nobel Peace Prize "for her nonviolent struggle for democracy and human rights" in Burma, now Myanmar. She gives her $1.3 million prize money to an education fund for the people of Burma.

Caution: Bullies Straight Ahead

Dealing with bullies is like dealing with any roadblock—you work your way around them. But beware: you can't always spot a bully by appearance. It's behavior that tells the story.

Take a look at the pictures above and pick out the bully. Then explain your choice.

. . . .

. . . .

. . . .

Guess what? Any one of these girls could be a bully! You can't judge a bully by how she looks. Even a girl who appears pretty, popular, and sweet can be a bully. You can tell if someone is a bully only by how she behaves. But few people act like bullies 100 percent of the time, and almost everyone has acted like a bully at one time. So instead of calling someone a bully, it's more accurate to say the person is "behaving" like a bully at a particular moment.

What is bullying behavior? Check all that apply:

_____ Spreading rumors   _____ Yelling

_____ Gossiping   _____ Excluding others

_____ Telling lies   _____ Giving the silent treatment

_____ Kicking   _____ Calling names

_____ Keeping secrets   _____ Hitting

_____ Eye-rolling   _____ Manipulation

If you checked all of the above, you're correct! The traditional image of a bully is a big, burly kid who physically intimidates and hurts others. But bullying isn't just physical. Bullies terrorize in other ways that can be more frightening—because they are less obvious. Bullies can be very creative in their cruelty—especially when they use some of the powerful strategies you have already encountered in this journey: cliques, hierarchies, secrets, gossiping, silent treatments, making up rumors, and excluding.

These bullying behaviors, which destroy friendships or social standing, are called *relational aggression*. Check out the story of "Carlie and the Roses" on the next page.

Carlie and the Roses

When Carlie walked over to the lunch table she had been eating at for months with her three best friends, she couldn't find a spot. The first empty chair she approached was "taken," according to Zahara. The other empty chair was piled up with all the girls' backpacks and no one made a move to clear it. Carlie felt embarrassment flood her face. No one said a word while she just stood there. The silence prompted Carlie to turn away and find another table.

A few days before that lunchtime snubbing, Carlie had gotten into an argument with Jessica—something about a phone call that hadn't been returned on time. She talked to Jessica about it during homeroom and thought everything was cool. But now this.

The Roses' Rules

Carlie attends high school in a quiet suburban town in Maryland. She doesn't think her group of friends is a clique, but her group has a name—the Roses. The Roses have rules that all the girls follow faithfully. The "color rule" is about wearing certain colors that are "in"—currently baby pink, dark purple, and gray. Black, that was required just a few months ago, is now "out" and off limits—even for shoes.

Another rule is about boys—they are classified by "date list," "buds list," and "loser list" (which is by far the longest). Carlie and her friends are not allowed to date anyone who is not on the "date list," and they cannot be friends with anyone not on the buds list.

The leader of the Roses is Jessica. Next in line is Ingrid, who seems to have almost as much power as Jessica. Carlie had thought that she and Zahara were equal in position—until all this happened. Carlie guesses that Jessica still hasn't forgiven her for arguing with her, and then she got the other girls to align themselves against her, too.

THE ROSES

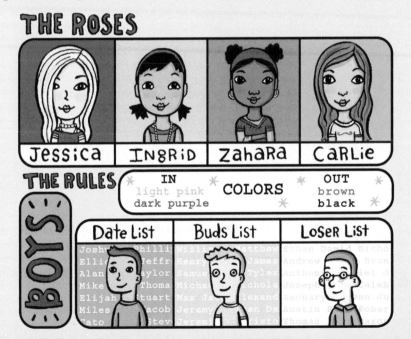

| Jessica | Ingrid | Zahara | Carlie |

THE RULES

BOYS

IN	COLORS	OUT
light pink		brown
dark purple		black

Date List	Buds List	Loser List
Joshu... Philli...	Willi... ...atthew	Ethan ...avid Nicho...
Elli... Jeffr...	Henry ...James	Andrew ...Bran...
Alan ...aylor	Samue... Tyle...	Anthon... ...iel J...
Mike ...Thoma...	Micha... ...ichola...	Joseph ...aleb
Elijah ...tuart	Max Ja... ...lexand...	Zachary ...an Ju...
Miles ...acob	Jeremy ...an Da...	Austin ...Rober...
...ato ...tev...	Jerem... ...risto...	Thomas ...axon

Things Get Weirder

During the next few days after the lunch table snub, things got weirder. None of the other girls spoke to Carlie unless she spoke first. They began sitting at a different lunch table and never invited Carlie. Torn between just joining them or asking them if she could join them, Carlie realized that neither choice was appealing. Going over and sitting down uninvited meant possible rejection. But asking permission would further lower her status in the group. The one time she tried to find out what was going on, Ingrid told her she was imagining things.

Then Carlie's friends started to take turns coming over to her and asking her silly questions in super-serious voices or passing her written notes. No matter what Carlie answered, the others took her note and passed it around in a fit of giggles. This made Carlie increasingly uncomfortable and, in the end, devastated her.

Photocopies of these notes, which seemed to have some sort of sexual implication, were plastered around the school—not in obvious places where teachers were likely to notice and pull them down immediately, but inside the girls' and boys' locker rooms and bathrooms, stuffed into random hallway lockers, and taped underneath desks in study hall. That's when Carlie knew a full-out war was on.

Thorns Come Out

Zahara had a Friday night sleepover, but Carlie wasn't invited. She found out about it when Jessica "accidentally" included her in a text message telling everyone what a great time she had had. At one point, a large number of the Roses' friends received an e-mail from an anonymous account with a list of ugly untruths about Carlie. As a result, Carlie stayed home from school for a week, miserable and in tears.

Carlie, who had spent much of her time and energy building friendships with Jessica, Zahara, and Ingrid, now found herself alone and lonely. She didn't have many other friends, partially due to the Roses' rules about not hanging out with "nonapproved girls."

Carlie is trying hard to overcome her fear of going to school, where her former friends continue to ignore and exclude her. Although she's encouraged that they appear to have stopped actively torturing her, she says, "I still really don't understand what happened and why all of them suddenly started to hate me. No one would tell me anything."

The Roses didn't physically hurt Carlie, but their actions were just as painful, especially because they seemed to have happened for no good reason. Feeling in need of new friends, Carlie went to a meeting of her school's International Society, a club the Roses made fun of. To her surprise, she found the club members interesting, friendly, and fun. They were not "oddball, creepy freaks," as Jessica used to call them. Carlie slowly began to realize that, in fact, the Roses, with their cruel and exclusionary tactics, were actually the creepy ones.

Circle all the types of bullying behavior that Carlie experienced:

If you were Carlie, how would you feel? What would you want her or someone else in the story (you can even add in a character) to do? What would you tell Carlie to do?

....

....

What kinds of bullying behavior do you see in your world?

List any times that you experienced relational aggression.	What did you do about it?	If you were not happy with the result, what could you try to do next time?

If you or someone you know is being bullied, here are some positive ways to help deal with the anxiety, loneliness, and stress:

Be safe

If you're concerned about your safety, immediately find an adult you can trust who will help you speak to parents, clergy, or school administrators about your situation.

Talk about it

Tell someone what's happening—a teacher or counselor, your parents, or other friends, and brainstorm some ideas on how to get out of the situation. If it's easier to write about it, put your thoughts in a letter or your journal and show that to an adult you trust. If you feel the situation is more serious than adults seem to think, keep at it. Sometimes adults need a reminder to stop and think, too.

Practice confidence

Work on ways to feel your best, and hold your head up high (even if you feel nervous at first). When you act like the teasing doesn't bother you and portray an image of strength, it helps keep others from teasing or picking on you.

Join a club

Make a new group of buddies by signing up for a club or organization that interests you. Or do some volunteer work—helping others often feels just as good as having someone help you.

Bullying Hurts Everyone

A bully usually targets someone. That person is sometimes called the "target." Someone who is present when bullying occurs is called a "witness." What role (bully, target, or witness) do you usually take in your life?

. . . .

Targets are more likely to:	Kids who bully are more likely to:	Witnesses who observe cruelty and feel powerless to help are more likely to:
• have learning problems • skip classes or drop out of school • lash out violently at classmates • attempt suicide	• become criminals involved in gangs • have employment difficulties • suffer mental health problems • struggle with alcohol and substance abuse • have higher rates of divorce	• have lifelong feelings of guilt and shame • suffer low self-esteem and quality of life

Instead of calling someone a bully, it's better to say that she is "behaving like a bully"—if you label the action, not the person, she will be more likely to "hear" you.

WITNESS, PLEASE!

> *No snowflake in an avalanche ever feels responsible.*
>
> *—Voltaire*

Witnesses are usually the most powerful people in a bullying situation. Statistics show that when a peer witness intervenes, bullying will stop in less than 10 seconds nearly 60 percent of the time. Witnesses have the power to prevent bullying from escalating, and to help stop it when it's happening.

What kind of a witness are you? Take a look at the definitions below. Then think about whether your behavior empowers you to stop bullying. If it does, what strategies have you used successfully in these situations? If it doesn't, what can you do to play a more active role in ending bullying?

TYPES OF WITNESSES

passive	sees the bullying but avoids the situation
fearful	afraid to help because the bully might turn on her
watcher	watches and maybe enjoys it, happy not to be the target
accomplice	laughs at the bully's abuse and becomes an appreciative audience
defender	challenges the bully or supports the victim

> **Which type of witness do you think more people should be?**
>
> ....
>
> ....

> **Which type of witness were you the last time you were in the presence of bullying behavior?**
>
> ....
>
> ....

FLIP THE SCRIPT: WITNESS POWER

Read the following scenarios with your friends. Identify the bully, the target, and the witness in each scenario. Then think up an ending for each scenario that gives the witness the power to change the situation.

SCENE A: LOCKER ROOM CHATTER

Just as Tara enters the locker room to get ready for soccer practice, she overhears a group of girls talking about how poorly she played in the last soccer game. They agree to not pass her the ball at all, and one of them, Billie, even says she's going to block Tara any chance she gets just to teach her a lesson. The truth is that Billie played the worst of everyone in the last game, but no one stands up to her because she's the team's most aggressive player. Tara turns toward her locker, making eye contact with Wendy, who has also overheard the entire conversation.

SCENE B: PHOTO QUEEN

Izzie, Lana, and Jeannie are all yearbook editors. Izzie, the photo editor, is trying to narrow down two final pages for today's photo deadline. The pages are filled with pictures she thinks are inappropriate, and all have one thing in common: Lana, the yearbook's editor-in-chief. When Izzie points out to Lana that it's inappropriate to have the editor-in-chief in so many photos, Lana is annoyed. She says the photos contain advertisements for some of the yearbook's largest sponsors. But Izzie can see that Lana is the focus of each photo and only a blurred background contains the sponsor's logo. Jeannie, who's editor of the clubs section, where the photos are going to appear, is torn between just including the photos to avoid irritating Lana and doing what's best for the yearbook.

SCENE C: LOCKER BLOCK

Cassie is leaning against some hall lockers talking with Enrique, making it impossible for Amy to get to her locker, which is between Cassie and Enrique. Cassie knows that Amy wants to get to her locker but doesn't bother to get out of the way. Amy has had to deal with this same situation in the past. All Cassie does is roll her eyes and move so that now she and Enrique are both leaning on Amy's locker. Shara is observing from three lockers down.

SCENE D: SILENT TREATMENT

Maya, Amber, and Lynn spent last weekend studying together for a geometry test. Maya knew the material least well of the three, but she got the highest grade on the test. She claims she's just naturally gifted when it comes to geometry, but Lynn knows that Amber is far better at math. Lynn asks Maya who she sat next to during the test. Maya gets angry because she understands Lynn is trying to say that she cheated off the person sitting next to her. Maya yells at Lynn to keep her mouth shut and mind her own business. Maya grabs Amber's arm and storms off. For the next week, Maya ignores Lynn, and Amber says hello to Lynn only when Maya isn't around.

SCENE E: IT HURTS — IN TEXT AND IN LIFE

A new animated film was out that sounded really cool, and Sandra was looking forward to seeing it with Lyla and Zemi over the weekend. They'd been talking about going to a movie all week. But Sandra didn't know that Lyla had been texting Zemi all morning about wanting to see the latest romantic comedy instead. Then, in biology class, Sandra was sitting with Zemi and saw the message that arrived from Lyla: "Don't let Sandra choose the movie. She always wants to see stupid animated films—they're 4 babies. I was sooooo :| last time." Zemi just shrugged her shoulders even though Sandra seemed hurt. Zemi rushed away as soon as class ended. Later, at lunch in the school cafeteria, Sandra tried to talk to Lyla. "I thought we all agreed to go see the new animated film." Lyla glared at Zemi and then quickly turned to Sandra. "Oh, just deal," she said. "You're such a baby. We're going to the chick flick. You'd better be there, and tell your mom she's driving." Zemi heard the conversation but couldn't think of anything to say, so she made a big deal about having to get to her next class early.

Speak Up and Report It! If you and your friends witness bullying, say something. To stay silent is to condone the behavior. Be a leader and stand up for the target.

DON'T FORGET: TATTLING IS ABOUT GETTING SOMEONE INTO TROUBLE, BUT REPORTING IS TRYING TO GET SOMEONE OUT OF TROUBLE.

Remember...

Bullying is usually a temporary situation. If you're being harassed, stand up for yourself (and ask friends to stand with you) to set the standard that bullying won't be tolerated. Do whatever it takes and find whatever help you can to get out of the situation.

Ever Been a BULLY?

Have you ever felt so much anger, powerlessness, or pain that you engaged in relational aggression or any other kind of bullying?

When you have a fight with your brother or sister, is it bullying?

Why or why not?

What happened?

Former bullies report that focusing on empathy (what the other person feels) made the biggest difference in their behavior. The next time you're tempted to lash out, try to take a minute to think about the other person's feelings. Also think about how you might feel if the situation were reversed.

**To-Do: Find a way to be kind to a bully.
Why might this be a good idea?**

"Just Kidding"

Has this ever happened to you?

Taína's example of kidding around:
"My cousin had a sleepover at her house where we watched horror movies and snacked on pizza. I was having a good time. Then my cousin's friend said to me, 'You smell like a garbage dump.' When I got mad, she said, 'I'm only kidding—you're supposed to laugh.' I don't get how that's supposed to be funny."

Sometimes bullies like to say, "Just joking!" or "Just kidding!" after they have said something mean. They think it gets them off the hook because it makes the target look like she can't take a joke or that she's a bad sport. But mean behavior is no joke—it's a form of bullying.

Here's a way to tell whether you are really joking, teasing, or bullying:

JOKING. Both of you are on the same level and are comfortable, laughing or giggling together.

TEASING. You treat your friend as if she is not on the same level. She becomes uncomfortable and wishes the teasing would stop. You may both be laughing, but her laughter may be forced. (Or you may have a friend who treats you this way.)

BULLYING. You are very uncomfortable and desperately wish she would stop. Laughter, name-calling, and rude language are directed at you. Maybe you are also getting shoved or pushed, or experiencing other physical force. (Or maybe *you* are doing the bullying.)

Try This with a Friend

Watch a movie, read a book, or surf the Internet together for more ideas about coping with bullying behavior. See if you come up with ideas you could adapt for a Take Action Project to make a difference! Here are a few ideas:

Movies
- "Bratz" (PG, 2007)
- "Bridge to Terabithia" (PG, 2007)
- "Simon Birch" (PG, 1998)
- "Ant Bully" (PG, 2006)

Books
- *Odd Girl Speaks Out: Girls Write about Bullies, Cliques, Popularity, and Jealousy,* by Rachel Simmons (Houghton Mifflin Harcourt, 2004)
- *Stick Up for Yourself: Every Kid's Guide to Personal Power and Positive Self-Esteem,* by Gershen Kaufman, Lev Raphael, and Pamela Espeland, revised and updated edition (Free Spirit Publishing, 1999)

Website
- Stop Bullying (www.stopbullying.gov)

Time with Your Trusted Adult

Talking about bullies and bullying behavior with someone you trust can make you feel a lot better about dealing with these nonpeaceful relationships. When you get together with your trusted adult, ask:

- Why do you think people bully? What do they gain?

- Have you ever dealt with a bully, either when you were a girl or as you've gotten older? If so, how did you handle it?

- In situations where bullies are involved, what role do you see me as—target, bully, or witness?

- If there's one piece of advice you'd give to someone being bullied, what would it be?

- How can you support me to be a role model when it comes to dealing with bullying behavior?

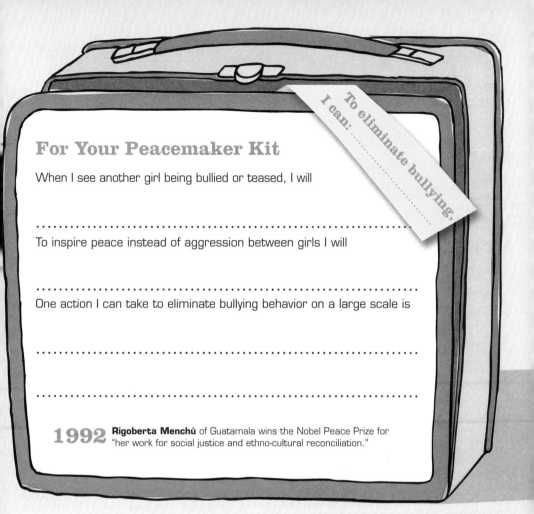

For Your Peacemaker Kit

When I see another girl being bullied or teased, I will

....

To inspire peace instead of aggression between girls I will

....

One action I can take to eliminate bullying behavior on a large scale is

....

....

**To eliminate bullying,
I can:** ....

1992 **Rigoberta Menchú** of Guatamala wins the Nobel Peace Prize for "her work for social justice and ethno-cultural reconciliation."

Take a Peace Break

Make a Zen Garden

A Zen garden is made to closely resemble the calm beauty in nature. Stones stand for mountains; soft moss in small pools of water can look like islands—especially with pebbles and sand around the moss. Use a shoebox lid, or anything like it, lined with wax paper. Design the sand, moss, and pebbles as you like so that the garden suits your sense of a calm scene. Rake the sand with a fork or small piece of cardboard to change the "paths" according to your mood.

Move Your Body

• • • • • • • • • • • • • •

Take a martial arts class, do yoga, play a sport, dance, go for a run, or work out at the gym. All of these will make you feel powerful, hone your concentration skills, and lift your sense of what you can do.

Yoga Move: Sun Salutation

The Sun Salutation is really 12 yoga poses that flow together and help increase your strength and flexibility. Check it out online by searching on "yoga and sun salutation," and give your muscles a challenge.

CONFIDENCE ROCKS!

Music has the power to heal and strengthen—so let it work for you! Create a playlist with songs that inspire you and fill you with confidence (remember that courage, confidence, and character are the three C's of Girl Scout leadership). Listen to your confidence playlist on the way to school or sing along to it at home.

Confidence (Courage and Character) Playlist

Song title	Artist	Favorite line

surfing through cyber-relationships

It's pretty amazing: You can go online, anytime, and connect with anyone anywhere in the world. When you spend time in chat rooms, social networking sites, and virtual worlds, you develop relationships—short-term or ongoing—with people you may never know in person.

These connections can enrich your mind—giving you new ideas and perspectives, and offering you opportunities to share yours.

Just because cyber-relationships are not "face 2 face" doesn't mean they don't require real skill to navigate them. You can get hurt—or do some hurting—via online connections. So here's to "netiquette" and some special tools to think about in your virtual word!

P.S.: Your family always knows which friends you are with and where you are, right? That's pretty important. And it applies to your online life, too. Let the adults at home know who you're meeting online. It's a little conversation that's good for your safety—and your family's peace of mind!

Letter of the (Girl Scout) Law!

Who are you when you are online? Does your online self measure up with who you really want to be?

"Netiquette" is the set of rules for how people treat each other online. And, hey, the Girl Scout Law is a great place to start when thinking about practicing good netiquette. Read through each line of the Girl Scout Law below and give an example or two of how your online behavior does or does not reflect these ideals. For example, have you ever:

been "unsisterly" when you sent a nasty message via IM without thinking it over first? Is it "easier" to be mean when you don't see the person?

shown disrespect by ignoring the rules set out by parents, teachers, and/or Internet service providers about bullying and harassment?

Values of the Girl Scout Law

I will do my best to be:

honest and fair ....

friendly and helpful ....

considerate and caring ....

courageous and strong ....

responsible for what I
say and do ....

and to:

respect myself and others ....

respect authority ....

use resources wisely ....

make the world a better place ....

be a sister to every Girl Scout ....

How are relationship rules online and offline the same?

How are they different?

How do you separate "friends" from online acquaintances?

How well do you need to know someone to accept them as your online "friend"?

Have you ever not accepted a friendship request?

How do you tell someone that you don't want to be their friend?

Cyber-Slammed

Have you ever gotten an intimidating IM from a classmate? Or maybe one of your friends has gotten not-nice cell phone messages from the class creep. It's the new reality: Bullies are no longer confined to the school yard! They've turned high-tech, using all the latest communication tools to inflict their bad behavior on targets.

And cyberspace offers bullies a whole new twist: They can now do a lot of their bullying anonymously, which means it's way too easy to go too far with what they say and do to others.

Cyber Solutions

If you've ever been cyber-bullied, you know how awful it can be. Or perhaps you've done some cyber-bullying yourself, texting without thinking or passing on some bit of info that you know is cruel. Either way, it's time to take action—and you can make a real difference.

 IMing, e-mailing, or texting rumors, gossip, or unflattering or doctored photos of someone or posting them on the Internet for everyone to see

 Using the Internet to give someone the cold shoulder by not answering her e-mails or instant messages

 Saying bad things about someone in a chat room or giving out her personal information

Do you have a real-life example of a time when you or someone you know got involved with cyber-bullying? What did you do?

....

....

....

....

Let Kindness Be Your Shield

Be part of the solution to cyber-bullying—be a positive force in cyberspace! Do a little targeted random act of kindness: Use your e-mail to send words of encouragement and positive comments to friends and family members. Remember: Messages sent by e-mail, IM, or text are instantaneous—once you click "send," the message can't be taken back! (Luckily, when sending good messages, there's no click regret!)

Did You Know?

The Girl Scouts surveyed 1,000 girls ages 13–18 and discovered:

Thirty percent said they'd been sexually harassed in a chat room.[1] *Wired News* reported that the harassment included unsolicited pictures and inappropriate demands for personal details.[2]

When asked how they know what is safe or unsafe behavior on the Internet, 84 percent cited their own common sense; 51 percent cited learning from parents; 46 percent cited television and the media; 29 percent cited teachers; 29 percent cited friends; and 4 percent said, "Nothing is that bad online because it is not really real."[1]

What would you say?

. . . .

. . . .

. . . .

[1] Whitney Roban, PhD, *The Net Effect: Girls and New Media* (Girl Scouts Research Institute, 2002)

[2] Noah Schachtman, "Scouts Survey Net Harassment" (*Wired News*, February 14, 2002)

How Safe Is

When you're online, you usually know who you're "talking" to. But sometimes you don't, and how you interact in those instances really matters—particularly for your safety. Test your cyber-safety savvy:

What makes a Web site reliable?

a) A friend recommended it.

b) It has tons of interesting links.

c) It looks very professional.

d) The URL ends in .edu or .gov.

If someone sends you their picture online, then you can feel safe talking with them, since you know what they look like.

Circle one: Fact   Myth

You are being followed from chat room to chat room by a person you met online. They are sending you IMs that make you uncomfortable. What should you do?

a) IM the person to leave you alone.

b) Log off immediately and tell a trusted adult that someone is harassing you.

c) Give the person some information they want so they will stop bugging you.

d) Feed the person fake information, just as a joke.

What's the best rule to follow for choosing your online name?

a) Use your real name.

b) Make up a name like cutehottie22 to get lots of responses.

c) Create a name that's not personal, like Aqua123.

d) Invent a name that says something personal about you, like Shygirl13.

CYBERSPACE?

It's safe to post a personal profile about yourself online because it can be seen only by your friends.

Circle one: Fact   Myth

5

You should never meet someone you've met online in a private place or at home alone.

Circle one: Fact   Myth

6

Cyber Quiz Answers

1 None of the Above! Just because a site ends in .edu (meaning it's connected with an educational institution) or .gov (it's connected with the government) doesn't mean the information is correct. A reliable Web site posts:

  a) the organization's name
  b) the author's name
  c) a way to contact the author
  d) a list of references

2 Myth. A photo can be a fake. Someone claiming to be a 14-year-old girl could be a 50-year-old man! Never get together with anyone you have met online without having a parent or other trusted adult with you.

3 B. If someone is IMing you and asking you for personal information or questions that make you uncomfortable, *don't respond.* You don't have to communicate with anyone you don't want to, and you should *never* give out personal information. If someone continues to harass you each time you log on, tell your parents, and have them contact your Internet provider to report the person who is bothering you. If the person is messaging you with details about yourself, like they know what you are wearing or what you ate yesterday at the mall or where you live, report it to the police.

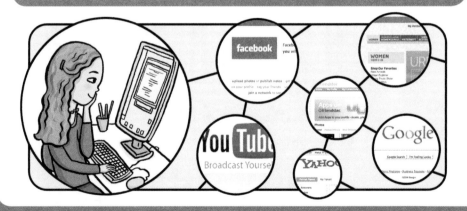

C. Create a name that's *not* personal. If the name is already taken, add some numbers to it. If you give yourself a suggestive name like cutehottie22, people may get the wrong idea about you, or judge you by your online name. If your name reveals something personal about you, like ShygirlNJ13, people may prey on that knowledge. *Don't use your real name, your real age, or your hometown.* A stranger can put two and two together to figure out who you are and where you live.

Myth. Anything you post online—even in a so-called "private" area—can be seen by almost anyone, including your parents or guardians, your teachers, your future bosses, and strangers. Even information that seems harmless (like what mall you shop at) could be used by a stranger to find you. Photos of yourself can be passed around and used in completely different contexts—ones you may not be happy about.

Fact. If someone you met online wants to meet you in person, contact your parents, guardian, or another trusted adult immediately. It is possible that you are being targeted by a sexual predator.

Improve Your Cyber Safety

For more information on how to prevent cyber-bullying before it happens or to report it when it does, visit www.stopbullying.gov/cyberbullying.

Take a moment to read over the Girl Scout Internet Safety Pledge on pages 110 and 111 of this book. Then sign it and show it to your friends and family. Ask if they want to take the Pledge too. Cyber safety is best when shared by all!

So Many Choices!

You and your friends are part of the most plugged-in generation in the history of planet Earth. Have you ever thought about the number of communication tools you use to maintain your relationship? Or the number of times you use them? You may be surprised at just how connected you are! Check all the communication tools that you use:

_____ Text messages

_____ Picture messages

_____ Video messages

_____ Voice messages

_____ E-mail

_____ Instant messages

_____ Chat rooms

_____ Online forums

_____ Other _____

_____ Other _____

BLOG

LOL :D

For one week, keep track of how many times you use just three of the communication tools listed. Now get out your calculators! Divide the number you just totaled by 7 to find out how many times a day on average you use each tool—and then multiply that number by 365 to find out how many times per year you use each. *Wow*—it's probably a much bigger number than you could have imagined! You really work hard at maintaining your relationships.

Communication Tool	Times Used per Week								Divided by 7 = Average # of Times Used per Day	Multiply by 365	Average # of Times per Year
	S	M	T	W	Th	F	S	= Total			
Text Message									÷7 =	x 365 =	
Instant Message									÷7 =	x 365 =	
E-mail									÷7 =	x 365 =	

Sometimes you can say something in person without causing hurt or conflict. But put that same message into an e-mail or a text message, and you might cause a big misunderstanding. The tone of your voice or the way you lift your eyebrows or soften the message with a hand gesture can convey that you mean no harm. But in cyberspace, there are no such nuances.

So when you have something really important to say, real life is almost always better than virtual.

Emoticons are a fun way to convey a little more of your meaning when communicating in cyberspace. Check out these and invent some new ones with your friends.

Symbol	Meaning
:		How boring . . .
:-o	Oh no!
:-D	Ha-ha!
#-o	Duh!
: -)	Big smile . . .
{: [	I'm mad!
:-(	Boo hoo!
;-)	Wink! Wink!
Create your own . . .	

VIRTUAL

LIVE VS

Time with Your Trusted Adult

With new technologies popping up every day, you may know more about digital communication than your trusted adult. When you get together, talk about how you use technology, and maybe even show her a few tips for staying connected.

Ask: What's your opinion of technological communication and its impact on relationships? Has there been a time when you didn't feel safe online? If so, how did you get out of the situation?

Make a commitment to this Internet Safety Pledge and ask your friends, and their friends, to make the commitment, too—and pass it on!

- I will not give out personal information such as my address, telephone number, parents' work address/telephone number, or the name and location of my school without my parents' permission.

- I will tell my parents right away if I come across any information that makes me feel uncomfortable.

- I will never agree to get together with someone I "meet" online without first checking with my parents. If my parents agree to the meeting, I will be sure that it is in a public place and I'll bring my parent or guardian along.

- I will never send a person my picture or anything else without first checking with my parents.

- I will not respond to any messages that are mean or in any way make me feel uncomfortable. It is not my fault if I get a message like that. If I do, I will tell my parents right away so that they can contact the Internet service provider.

- I will talk with my parents so that we can set up rules for going online. We will decide upon the time of day that I can be online, the length of time I can be online, and appropriate areas for me to visit. I will not access other areas or break these rules without their permission.

- I will never open an e-mail from someone I don't know or click on links I don't recognize.

- I will not give out my Internet password to anyone (even my best friends) other than my parents.

- I will not go into chat rooms unless my parents say it's OK.

I will check with my parents before downloading or installing software or doing anything that could possibly hurt our computer or jeopardize my family's privacy.

I will be a good online citizen and not do anything that hurts other people.

I will help my parents understand how to have fun and learn things online and teach them things about the Internet, computers, and other technology.

I agree to the above terms.

. . . .
Your Name   Date

I will help my child follow this agreement and will allow reasonable use of the Internet, as long as these rules and other family rules are followed.

. . . .
Parent/Guardian   Date

Let Peace Begin With You

Let there be peace on earth
And let it begin with me;
Let there be peace on earth,
The peace that was meant to be.
> *— Jill Jackson and Sy Miller,*
> *"Let There Be Peace on Earth"*

This song, now known around the world, was written as a wish for world peace and what individuals could do to achieve it. It was first introduced at a summer retreat in the mountains of California, where 180 teens of varied religious, racial, cultural, and economic backgrounds met to create understanding and friendship through education, discussion groups, and living and working together in a camp situation.

You've been winding your way through a maze of first impressions and stereotypes, friendship joys and dilemmas, cliques, conflicts, and bullies. Perhaps you've tried an "I-statement" or two to express your real feelings in a powerful and positive way. Or maybe you've tried a week (or more) without gossiping. Maybe you've even stopped bullying someone—or stopped letting someone bully you.

Can you see how these actions impact more people than just yourself? Imagine your world if everyone were striving to do better with some of this relationship stuff at the same time. World peace? Well, the world would be a whole lot closer. (And you do have 2.6 million Girl Scout friends to start with!)

So here's your chance to be a leader. Grab some of the ideas and tips you've been gathering in aMAZE and bring them out into the world! Create a Take Action Project that engages others in your world in improving relationships. And while you're at it, try to get people to keep on "passing it forward."

First, take a moment to consider what being a leader means to you:

Defining a Real Leader

What values have you discovered about yourself that are also important to you as a leader?

What are your greatest strengths in connecting with others?

What ideas do you have about using your values and relationship skills to take action to change the world around you—even in a small way?

Diplomat Award

You earn your Diplomat Award by being a leader who brings a Take Action Project to life through these seven steps:

1. Identify a relationship issue you want to take action on.

2. Brainstorm a solution.

3. Assess your resources.

4. Create a realistic plan, including a time line.

5. Spread the word.

6. Carry out your Take Action Project.

7. Reflect on your project's results.

You can use these same steps and planning tools for any Take Action Project—whether in Girl Scouts or anytime in life.

Identify Your Issue and
Brainstorm a Solution

There's so much going on in the maze of friendships. How do you find an issue that others in your world really need to deal with, too? And once you grab the issue, what solutions might you create?

Here are a few ways to get you thinking about what a "Diplomat" Take Action Project might look like.

Organize a "mini-maze" workshop (or two or 10) for younger girls, at a school, within Girl Scouting, at your place of worship, or wherever else you belong where you can guide younger girls to better interactions! Take some of the examples you have used on your way through aMAZE and adjust them so they are engaging and meaningful for younger girls. Add some fun sparks, and off you go.

Can you think of a closing that invites the girls to also pass on to others something they learn from you? Or maybe your school or an organization you belong to can set this workshop up and offer it once a year—even after you're out of the picture.

If younger girls knew more about…

they would be better able to…

even before they leave elementary school…

and we might even…

If more people at our school would just…

then we would all be more…

Squelch the gossip urge? Mix it up every Friday in the lunchroom cafeteria? Trade seats on the bus? Give witness to bullying behavior? Stop enjoying jokes rooted in stereotypes? Show friends how much they are admired?

Ask around. If there is one "interact" issue that other kids at school want to deal with, what would it be? Start there. Then brainstorm what it is that could get the snowball rolling—a clever "advertising campaign" within school? Small group workshops? Monthly theme dates such as Unmatching Day or Come Dressed as Crazy Quilted as Can Be? No one can make fun of anyone? Open mike night—only poems, songs, dances that show positive interactions are featured? Who would you need to support you (school staff, PTA)? Start talking to them. And as long as you are talking, don't just ask for support with one event—how can you get a whole chain reaction going?

What is it that adults don't quite get about what you and your friends need? Maybe they don't really see how bad some of the bullying behaviors are? Maybe what you see as a big problem they see as a small one, so they don't really take the time to help you think it through? Why not create a play that in a humorous way shows adults what you need a little more of? Design a training workshop that adults in your Girl Scout council could participate in. Just remember, adults (like kids) will engage in your ideas best when your workshop is presented with tons of respect.

If the adults in our lives could just understand a little better about what we are going through in the maze of relationships, they could give us better support and advice.

It would be really great if adults...

then we would all be more...

and we might even...

SOME MORE IDEAS

Does your local library offer programming for kids your age or younger? As a Take Action Project, you could offer some events that engage kids in better navigating their maze of relationships.

Partner with a trusted adult and together run a friendship advice column for a local or school-based newspaper or radio station.

Work with friends to create short skits about the differences between friendship circles and cliques, during which you also provide ideas about how to exit peacefully from a cliquish situation. Perform these skits for younger girls. Work with your adult volunteer, an elementary school teacher, or a Brownie or Junior adult volunteer to plan a time when you can share the skits with the girls and discuss these issues further.

Perhaps you have an idea about "going bigger" with one of your Interact Challenge efforts. Did you spark something you could Take Action on in a more powerful and planned way?

How Two Girls Took Action "On the Road"

Kyldra and Jade were sick of watching all the bullying on the playground, in the lunchroom, and even in the halls at school. They decided that if younger kids learned some of the antibullying skills they had learned, maybe the bullying wouldn't happen so much. So they decided to make up a skit, practice it in front of other Girl Scouts, and then take it "on the road" to area fourth- and fifth-graders. Here's an excerpt:

Location:
LUNCHROOM

KYLDRA
(in excited, breathy way):
It happened again. That bully Bruno spilled his whole enchilada and milk tray all over Marcella's lunch and shirt! Well, Marcella had had enough and she flung her lunch bag at Bruno.

JADE
(gasps):
Oh no! I bet I know what happens next.

KYLDRA
(not waiting for Jade to guess):
Just then, the principal came in and the only thing she saw was Marcella flinging her bag at Bruno. So Marcella's the one who got detention!

JADE
(with hesitation):
You're going to tell the principal what really happened, aren't you?

KYLDRA
(softly):
I didn't see anything.

Kyldra and Jade followed up their skit by having a discussion with the kids in the audience. They used questions like these as prompts:

- Why was Kyldra afraid to talk about what she saw?
- Why would it be important for Kyldra to speak up?
- What would you do if you saw what happened between Bruno and Marcella?

They also passed out a printed list of antibullying skills. The skit, the discussion, and the list were so well-received that two other girls, Eliza and Seika, put on a similar skit at their community center. Two more Girl Scouts, Jill and Tahnisha, did the same with a group of Girl Scout Juniors. The bullying didn't stop right away, but the "Road Skit" slowly began to turn the tide. The girls found that simply raising awareness about bullying led to better relationships in their school and community.

HOW WILL YOU IMPROVE YOUR WORLD?

Write down any relationship problems in the world around you that you might like to take action on. Include any ideas you have, no matter how outrageous, to get other people involved in solving the issue. Solutions come in all sizes—large and small. Write them in the spaces below—and don't hold back!

ISSUE AREA	POSSIBLE SOLUTION	PPR	SAP	DO	LAW	FUN
1.						
2.						
3.						
4.						
5.						
6.						
7.						
8.						

PPR, SAP, DO, LAW, and FUN stand for each of the key elements that will contribute to your Take Action Project's success. Take a minute to put checks under the "keys to success" for each of the solutions, so that you can determine if this project:

Is fun—
and exciting to work on. Do you like telling other people about it?

Solves a problem
that's important to you and your community (Girl Scouts, school, place of worship, city, a local group, etc.).

Is doable,
when you look at the project's size and scope and the amount of time you have. "Smaller" can be better if it means you can really feel good about some accomplishments!

Lasts a while.
Even though the time you can spend may be short, you might be able to think of a way to set up your project so that some aspect of it has some staying power. Maybe it can be repeated on an annual basis. Maybe those you do it with will commit to pass one aspect or message forward. You get the idea—ongoing is always better than one time when you are working to Change the World!

Promotes peaceful relationships:
Does it establish positive connections between people?

Which of your projects had the most checks? Which had the second most? The third? Hey, look—you've suddenly narrowed down not just your topics, but your solutions, too!

The topics with the most checks are the ones that you will most likely enjoy and be able to feel a sense of accomplishment from. (If this is a team effort, conduct a vote on each of the problems and come to a consensus or general agreement. Tally up the checkmarks from each girl's book for each project to get a total number for the group.)

Using what you've learned from the exercises above, fill in the blanks below.

My (or my team's) Take Action Project will solve the problem of

by providing

This project will serve:

It strives toward being sustainable or is sustainable because:

Assessing Your RESOURCES

People are your greatest resource for bringing ideas to life! So before you jump in and build a project plan and time line, think about who else you will involve. Then think about what other materials you might need. Your answers might change your solution a little (or lead you to go back to Step 1) to make sure you end up with a project that's totally doable!

What are the main actions to do to make your project a reality?

1. ....

2. ....

3. ....

4. ....

5. ....

Who can help you with these actions? Who will contact these people and ask them if they are willing to help?

....

....

Are there any other organizations or groups you can invite to collaborate with you on this project? Who else might care about this issue with you? Who will contact these groups and find out about partnering up?

....

....

Potential partners

....

....

....

Putting Actions into a
Plan and Time Line

Now, put the list of actions you started creating into some order—step by step. Remember to look at your school calendars, national holidays, seasonal weather conditions, and any other factors that might impact how you choose to do your project.

Hint: Just as with mazes, it can be useful to start with the end date and make a time line working back from that date.

Task	Person Responsible	Date Needed

DOES YOUR PLAN INVOLVE

Say you've decided to offer a workshop on relationship-building techniques. One of the steps in your plan might be organizing what will go on during the workshop to make it a success. Use these tips to make sure you offer a workshop that makes people say, "Wow!"

Goals. What is the workshop about? Why does it matter? What are the one or two things you want everyone who participates to walk away knowing, doing, or feeling? Remember, people can only absorb so much—to make an impact, zoom in on just a few ideas and then get creative about how you convey them!

Opener. What will you say or do at the very beginning to get everyone sitting up and taking notice? How will they know that what you have to share is really going to matter to them?

ORGANIZING A WORKSHOP?

Breaking the ice. What short activity can you get everyone doing together that creates the feeling that you are all a team during this workshop? If people don't know each other at all, this might include a fun way for some introductions to take place.

Feeling safe. Depending on the topics and exercises, you might want to lead the group to make a team agreement. Does what happens here stay here? Will personal examples or feelings be shared? What do participants need to promise each other to feel comfortable?

The main action. Dive into whatever the purpose of the workshop is. Everyone learns best when there is some doing—not just listening—involved.

Gather up the insights. Based on the activity and discussion, what do people think now? How does this apply to their lives? What might they do differently?

Now what? What are you inviting people to "go forth" and do or change? Be specific. Give them all the information or tools they will need. What will make the effort you started keep going and growing?

SPREAD THE WORD

How can your Take Action Project be a success if no one knows about it? *It can't!* So get people in your school or community looped in. You and your friends are probably already masters of publicity—and you may not even know it! Telling your friends about important things is the first step in publicity. For your Take Action Project, you need to turn the communication skills you use with your friends out into the greater community.

Depending on the project you are doing, it could be that you want publicity before the event or after the event—or maybe you need both. So, notice that Step 5 might actually be happening while you are simultaneously actually starting the project (Step 6).

What Captures Your Imagination?

Think about advertisements that make you stop and think. What makes them successful? What can you apply to your efforts to get the word out? And when it comes to words, notice how sometimes "less is more." What are the fewest, most important things you want to convey about your project?

What ways are available in your community to get the word out? Web sites? Newspapers? Radio stations? Bulletin boards? Who runs these things? How could they help you?

Word of mouth is a powerful way to get people looped in. Can you think of a fun way to get the people you need involved to pass the message along?

Publicity Ideas

If you are a little stuck for creativity at the moment, here are a few examples to build on.

- Spend an afternoon calling people and checking out places that are best suited for promoting your project.

- Check out the best places to put up posters or fliers. (You might want to spend some time before the walk-around creating fliers and posters to promote your project so you have samples to show businesses.)

- Send an e-mail or text blast to your contacts.

- Write an article or post a blog for your local newspaper or community newsletters to give people an idea of what you're working on.

As your plan takes shape, you can organize it like this:

Publicize It

Action Needed	Person Responsible	Date
Call potential partners		
Send an e-mail/text blast		
Create posters/fliers		
Hang posters in business windows		
Write an article/post a blog		
Come up with a crazy contest		

You're Ready, You're Set, Now GO!

It's the moment you've been working and waiting for! All you need to do is put your project into action. Use the space above to list any loose ends and last-minute details that you need to attend to to make your Take Action Project a success!

analyze THIS:
Sadie and Zelna's "No-Ridicule Zone"

What do you think? Could "No-Ridicule Zones" work everywhere?
Check out this example and see how the "7-Step Plan" is used—or not!

Sadie and Zelna complained to their Girl Scout adviser: "We can't get away from it. Kids are always teasing each other and bullying and embarrassing other kids all the time. They try to see who can say the wildest thing. And it's usually the same kids—over and over—who are the butt of all the bullying."

Zelna and Sadie complained so much that they decided to try an idea they saw on a Web site. They would set up "No-Ridicule Zones" all over the school. With Girl Scout friends helping, the girls figured out a plan:

Zelna got three of the best artists she knew at school to help make signs. Two of them made great cartoon figures to label where the No-Ridicule Zones would be. The girls figured that a little humor would be much better than a "preachy" approach. One monkey character on a No-Ridicule Zone sign was standing on its head with tape over its mouth (not too tight) next to the words *Absolutely No Ridicule Allowed*.

Sadie and Zelna also walk home together from the school bus every day, and somehow the sounds of teasing in their neighborhood reached their ears and made them realize they needed to take their No-Ridicule idea further. They had to widen their reach—and soon.

"Maybe we can ask the dry cleaning and deli managers if we could put up our signs for 'No-Ridicule Zones' there, too," Zelna suggested.

Sadie agreed: "If it works at one place, it should work everywhere!"

What do you think? Could "No-Ridicule Zones" work everywhere?

....

....

REFLECT: HOW'D IT GO?
WHAT DID YOU LEARN?

Wow! So now you did it—you identified a problem, designed a solution, and put it into action. You're aMAZing!

Now that you've accomplished your Take Action Project, it's time to reflect back on it. Look at the successful steps you took and also the challenges you encountered. What might you do differently the next time you do something to change your world?

Successful Steps   What made it a success?

Challenges   How can it be overcome next time?

Now that you've accomplished your project, how do you feel? Write or draw how you're feeling.

How has your project spread some peace potential into your world?

What did other people say to you about your project?

HOW FeeLINGS FIT INTO
FarM WORK

Elizabeth Byanjeru Rubaihayo of Uganda is a scientist—an agricultural researcher—but her pioneering work relies on basic relationship strategies: good communication, understanding, and a personal touch. In her country, the majority of crop production, domestic and commercial, is done by women. So agricultural priorities are based on women's needs.

Rubaihayo's innovative crop research, which has brought health and economic benefits to her country and won prestigious awards, relies on her good relationships with female farmers and farm workers. Female researchers, she says, naturally use their interpersonal skills as they make technological improvements applicable to real women's lives.

PASS IT FORWARD

Congratulations. You're about to emerge from the maze of aMAZE! Think back to some of those relationship equations that got you started on this amazing journey:

Me=limitless possibilities.

You=limitless possibilities + another viewpoint

Me + You = interactions of boundless possibilities^2

Me + You x Both Our Networks = Diplomats^{10}

Diplomats^{10} x Millions More Around the World = Peace on the planet, or at least a far better world

> *A journey is best measured in friends, rather than miles.*
>
> —*Tim Cahill*
>   *adventure travel writer*

You've wound your way through some amazing twists and turns and roadblocks. And none of them stopped you from taking action toward a more peaceful world. You're truly a diplomat.

How would you like to talk one-on-one with a really famous world diplomat—a world peacemaker? Suppose you were given an hour to talk with a Nobel Peace Prize winner.

You've read about many peacemakers in this book, and many Nobel Prize winners. There are many more throughout the world. Who would you choose to talk with? What would you ask? What would you hope to gain from your discussion? Can you imagine winning the Nobel Peace Prize one day? If so, what would you want to win it for?

Celebrate!

Share your aMazing new insights with a Girls' Night In. Plan a sleepover or pizza party where you can all be yourselves and celebrate what makes you such great friends.

You've accomplished a lot through aMAZE and a festive celebration is the perfect reward! Remind each other that good leaders love to celebrate! They share the good times with the people most important in their lives. Capture some memories, too—create a photo-collage of the party night.

You can up the fun factor by giving your celebration a theme. Here are some ideas:

A Costume Party. Guests pair up and come as "famous friendships duos"—or as relationship obstacles (envy, gossip, silent treatment).

Get Silly. Have a little fun while reinforcing the truth that the "rules" in and around cliques are really pretty silly! Make up your own silly rules that everyone follows during all or part of your gathering. For example:

- **Everytime someone says "good," she has to eat a marshmallow.**

- **Only single earrings allowed—no pairs.**

- **You can't use your hands to eat.**

Let every guest make up one (nonharmful) rule. Give an award for the silliest, most giggle-inducing rule! Just remember, in a game, with true friends, no one feels ridiculous.

Get Serious. Together write a cinquain that expresses something you have learned from this journey. A cinquain is a poem with five lines:

1. one word (noun) as a title
2. two adjectives about the title
3. three verbs about the title
4. a four-word phrase describing a feeling related to the title
5. one word referring back to the title

....

....

....

....

....

Check out these examples:

Annette

caring, loyal

chatting, giving, sharing

looks out for me

friend

— Lacey, age 12

Leader

brave, compassionate

stands, speaks, achieves

interacts with peaceful gestures

me

— Bella, age 15

Thank Your Trusted Adult

Share your pride of accomplishment and some inspirational words about how you will continue to build peaceful relationships in the world around you:

- Write your trusted adult a thank-you note, expressing what you enjoyed most about being able to talk with her throughout the journey. Mail it to her.

- Take her to lunch to celebrate and thank her for being part of your support system on this journey.

- Plan a regular meeting place and time where you can continue to get together to talk about the relationships in your life (and hers).

- Share this aMAZE book with her and ask her to share her thoughts about the changes she saw in you, and ways she'll support you as you continue to build peaceful relationships as a leader.

Careers

Your interpersonal skills can lead to cool careers! Here are some to think about:

Actor Crisis negotiator **Customer service representative Diplomat or ambassador District sales manager** Entertainer **FBI profiler Financial adviser Guidance counselor** Hotelier **Interviewer Translator/interpreter Legal adviser** Mediator **Personal trainer Politician Psychologist** Public relations agent **Salesperson School counselor Social worker** Talk-show host **Teacher Tour guide**

I completed the aMAZE leadership journey:

Date:

. . . .

How I can commit to interact with others, practice diplomacy, and be a peacemaker beyond aMAZE:

. . . .

. . . .

. . . .

Discovering Myself

I can be myself in friendships by

. . . .

I discovered that I can steer clear of peer pressure by

. . . .

ENTER ➡

Connecting with Others

Healthy friendships are founded on

interact

. . . .

I can nurture friendships in my world by

. . . .

. . . .

Taking Action

I learned I can be a diplomat when I take action to:

diplomat

. . . .

. . . .

. . . .

. . . .

Peacemaker Award

If all girls were involved in peaceful
relationships, how would the world be different?

. . . .

. . . .

The most important tools in my Peacemaker Kit are

. . . .

. . . .

I commit to using these tools to

. . . .

. . . .

EXIT →

An Amazing End to an Amazing Journey

Take a look at the poem below. Now that you've journeyed through aMAZE, how does this poem resonate with you?

A Maze Me

Life is a tangle of
twisting paths.
Some short.
Some long.

There are dead ends.
And there are choices.
And wrong turns,
and detours,
and yield signs,
and instruction booklets,
and star maps,
and happiness,
and loneliness.
And friends.
And sisters.
And love.
And poetry.

Life is a maze.
You are a maze.
Amazed.
And amazing.

By Naomi Shihab Nye, from A Maze Me:
Poems for Girls (Reprinted with permission
Naomi Shihab Nye © 2005 HarperTeen)

Some people come into our lives and quickly go.
Some stay for a while, leave footprints on our hearts,
and we are never, ever the same.

— Flavia Weedn

"Stay" is a charming word in a friend's vocabulary.
— *Louisa May Alcott*